Start Your Own

WEDDING CONSULTANT BUSINESS

Additional titles in *Entrepreneur's* Startup Series

Start Your Own

Arts and Crafts Business
Automobile Detailing Business
Bar and Club
Bed and Breakfast
Blogging Business
Business of eBay
Business Support Service
Car Wash
Child-Care Service
Cleaning Service
Clothing Store and More
Coaching Business
Coin-Operated Laundry
Construction and Contracting Business
Consulting Business
Crafts Business
Day Spa and More
e-Business
e-Learning Business
Event Planning Business
Executive Recruiting Business
Fashion Accessories Business
Florist Shop and Other Floral Businesses
Food Truck Business
Freelance Writing Business and More
Freight Brokerage Business
Gift Basket Service
Grant-Writing Business
Graphic Design Business
Green Business

Growing and Selling Herbs and Herbal
 Products
Hair Salon and Day Spa
Home Inspection Service
Import/Export Business
Information Consultant Business
Information Marketing Business
Kid-Focused Business
Mail Order Business
Medical Claims Billing Service
Net Services Business
Online Education Business
Personal Concierge Service
Personal Training Business
Pet Business and More
Pet-Sitting Business and More
Photography Business
Public Relations Business
Restaurant and More
Retail Business and More
Self-Publishing Business
Seminar Production Business
Senior Services Business
Specialty Travel and Tour Business
Staffing Service
Tutoring and Test Prep Business
Vending Business
Wedding Consultant Business
Wholesale Distribution Business

Entrepreneur
MAGAZINE'S

start*up*

3RD EDITION

Start Your Own

WEDDING CONSULTANT BUSINESS

Your Step-by-Step Guide to Success

Entrepreneur Press and Eileen Figure Sandlin

EP
Entrepreneur.
Press

Entrepreneur Press, Publisher
Cover Design: Beth Hansen-Winter
Production and Composition: Eliot House Productions

This publication is designed to provide accurate and authoritative information in regard to the subject
matter covered. It is sold with the understanding that the publisher is not engaged in rendering legal,
accounting or other professional services. If legal advice or other expert assistance is required, the services
of a competent professional person should be sought.

Library of Congress Cataloging-in-Publication Data
  Sandlin, Eileen Figure.
    Start your own wedding consultant business/by Entrepreneur Press and Eileen Figure
  Sandlin.—3rd ed.
    p.   cm.
  ISBN-13: 978-1-59918-427-2 (alk. paper)
  ISBN-10: 1-59918-427-3 (alk. paper)
    1. Wedding supplies and services industry—Management. 2. Consulting firms—Management.
  3. New business enterprises—Management. I. Entrepreneur Press. II. Title.
  HD9999.W372S26 2011
  392.5068—dc22   2011022058

Printed in the United States of America

15 14 13 12   10 9 8 7 6 5 4 3 2 1

Contents

Chapter 4

Chapter 5

Chapter 6

Appendix
Wedding Consultant Resources 157

Preface to the
Third Edition

It was a time when wedding consultants competently went about their business, creating sumptuous reception menus, ordering beautiful floral arrangements, and managing complex guest lists. Yet the first decade of the 21st century ushered in seething change. A deep recession decimated discretionary income and slashed property values. Two wars sent oil prices soaring. Social media created a new language and transformed how people communicate and interact.

Yet through this time of turmoil, one thing remained constant: Couples continued to marry—there were more than

2 million weddings in each year of the last decade—and wedding consultants continued to coordinate many of the events heralding these nuptials. These affairs may not have been the lavish events of previous times, but they still involved myriad details and planning—the type of planning at which wedding consultants excel.

However, to say that wedding consulting is a recession-proof industry would be naïve. The industry witnessed a drop in wedding budgets and a reduced demand for wedding consulting services in those recessionary times. But even in the darkest times, about 30 percent of bridal couples still engaged the services of a wedding planner. In addition, according to The Wedding Index, a survey that monitors the health of the wedding industry, spending on wedding products and services was up 23 percent in 2010 over the previous year, and survey respondents had great expectations for 2011 and beyond.

These are positive signs for both the wedding industry as a whole and for you in particular as you embark on a new career as a wedding consultant. There's no doubt that some brides will believe the many websites, blogs, and articles that claim that every woman is a closet time-management-and-planning genius who can flawlessly coordinate all the details related to a dream wedding, while juggling the demands of a career, and enjoying those special pre-wedding moments with the groom-to-be. Other brides who value their sanity will turn to a wedding coordinator to make sure everything goes off without a hitch.

Making sure your new business gets off on the right foot is the goal of the book you're holding. It provides all the practical advice you need to build the foundation for a wedding consulting business and launch it efficiently. Included is the 411 about the many details involved in starting and operating a small business, from analyzing the market, writing a business plan, and establishing an internet presence to finding financing and handling all the other day-to-day duties necessary to keep a business running smoothly and profitably. In addition, it contains worksheets that will help you calculate your startup costs and keep your budget in line, as well as words of wisdom and tips from successful wedding consultants around the country. Just add a dash of determination, a dollop of good humor, and a drop of human kindness, and you'll have the right recipe to make your brides' and your own dreams come true.

Best wishes for a long and prosperous union!

Here Comes the Bride . . .
and the Wedding Consultant

Once upon a time on a perfect summer day, guests in colorful wedding finery filled an old cathedral. The fragrance of dew-kissed blossoms wafted through the air as melodious organ music played. A radiant bride walked up the aisle on the arm of her father to meet the handsome groom waiting at the altar . . .

Royal wedding or fairy tale? Neither. It's the perfect day every bride dreams of—and wedding consultants help to make those dreams come true.

The wedding industry is a $72 billion business, with nearly 542,000 businesses serving it, according to *The Wedding Report*, a provider of wedding statistics and market research for the industry. Those businesses run the gamut from bridal salons and tuxedo rental stores to florists, photographers, reception facilities, and, of course, wedding consultants.

Yet the wedding industry is not without its challenges. The first decade of the new millennium saw a decline in wedding spending during the darkest days of the recession. According to surveys by *The Wedding Report*, the average wedding cost $28,730 in 2007. By 2009, that figure had dipped to $19,580. But in 2010, wedding spending had risen nearly 19 percent to $24,070, and the outlook is bright again for the future.

Wedding consultants have had their own challenges as well, from the slow economy and a plethora of information available on the internet for determined DIYers to competition from wedding venues that offer complete bridal packages. But people will always get married—in fact, there were nearly 2.2 million marriages in 2009, according to the U.S. Census Bureau's "2011 Statistical Abstract of the United States." So even if the economy goes south again, many women, who are simply too busy juggling the demands of their professional and personal lives to oversee the multitude of details inherent in wedding planning, are still likely to have a wedding consultant on their wedding services shopping list.

The "2010 Real Weddings Survey," published by The Knot Inc., a lifestyle media company, bears this out. Results showed that nearly one-third used a wedding planner, and more than half those brides (52 percent) engaged a planner for wedding day coordination. Even the economic news wasn't quite as dire as you might think when it came to matters matrimonial. Fewer than one-third (31 percent) of the surveyed brides said that the economy impacted their wedding budget. Those who did feel the pinch compensated by reducing their guest list from an average of 149 guests in 2009 to 141 in 2010.

And there's even more potential good news, thanks to the echo boomers, the largest generation of young people since the 1960s. While it's true they're waiting longer to get married—the average marriage age is now 26.1 for women and 28.2 for men, according to the U.S. Census Bureau—experts are predicting that the wedding industry is on the brink of a new marriage boom that will bring many new opportunities for industry professionals like wedding consultants.

Since no one formally tracks the figures, it's difficult to pinpoint an exact figure for how many wedding consultant businesses there are nationwide. The best guess is approximately 10,000, a figure based on the number of people who pay for memberships to the various professional wedding associations, as well as the number of people on mailing lists available from list brokers. If you do the math—2.2 million possible opportunities annually for 100,000 wedding planners—you can see there's exciting potential for an aspiring wedding business owner like you.

Earnings Potential

Because wedding consultants are, in essence, independent contractors, it's hard to gauge how much a novice in the field can expect to earn, and what published information that does exist varies widely. What is known, however, is that the industry's standard fee is 15 percent of the wedding budget, although some consultants prefer instead to charge a flat fee for custom wedding packages they create. You'll find information about wedding packages in Chapter 2, "Here Comes the Wedding Consultant."

But some assumptions can be made about earnings potential. Robbi Ernst III, founder and president of June Wedding Inc., in Guerneville, Californina, says a novice consultant can usually coordinate 10 weddings a year. So if the average wedding budget is $24,000, as discussed earlier, that would yield a gross income of $36,000. Here's the math:

$$\$24,000 \times .15 = \$3,600 \times 10 \text{ weddings} = \$36,000$$

But, of course, not every bride will have that much to spend—and happily, some will have more. "The earnings potential for wedding consultants is awesome," says Richard Markel of the Association for Wedding Professionals International. "Those who are better connected and better educated will do the best in this business, as will those who network as a way to build their reputations."

Stat Fact
Research gathered by the Association of Bridal Consultants indicates that around 270,000 couples hire wedding planners each year. That equates to roughly 20 to 30 percent of all weddings that are coordinated by a wedding planning professional.

Profile of a Wedding Consultant

So what does it take to be a successful wedding consultant? Loreen Crouch, who owns a wedding consultant business in Ypsilanti, Michigan, says emphatically, "A

▲

sense of humor." And she's not kidding. In this business you're depending on the professionalism and reliability of up to a dozen or more people to create a bride's dream wedding. When dealing with so many vendors, there's always the possibility

An Eye for Trends

The wedding business is always changing as couples keep pushing the nuptial envelope, looking for imaginative ways in which to make their wedding special, unique, and memorable. A successful wedding consultant should have the ability to keep an eye on trends as they develop—and as they fade. Ann Nola of the Association of Certified Professional Wedding Consultants says these current wedding trends are "in":

- Private estates as wedding and reception sites
- Smaller wedding size as brides and grooms trim their lists, focusing on family, close friends, and longtime co-workers
- A return to formality
- Whimsical and colorful invitations
- Clever "save the date" reminders such as refrigerator magnets
- Theme-oriented weddings
- Monogram-themed weddings—everything from the invitations to the menus are adorned with the couple's monogram
- Small bridal parties
- Elegant bridal gowns as well as adding subtle color to the bride's gown
- Tuxedoes styled in a more suit-like fashion
- Table names instead of table numbers; for instance the tables might be named after a couple's favorite spots or favorite sports
- A trend toward personalization

Nola is based in California, so some of her trend-spotting may not apply to your area. However, she demonstrates through her keen observation the ability to stay on top of hot trends. Successful wedding planners will need to do the same in their locales.

that something will go askew or bomb out completely. That's why having a sense of humor and the ability to think fast on your feet are key to keeping things on track or fixing the problems that will inevitably crop up.

"I do laugh a lot, but that doesn't mean I'm taking anything lightly," Crouch says. "I'll put my foot down when necessary. But being warm and friendly puts clients who are tired and frustrated at ease, which makes my job easier."

In fact, being a people person is pretty much a requirement for this job. You'll be dealing constantly with weepy brides, demanding mothers, cranky suppliers, and others who are all vying for your attention at once. You'll be bargaining with vendors, overseeing the activities of hordes of hired helpers, and mingling with the guests at wedding receptions. So it helps if you really love working with people and have an upbeat, positive outlook that will help you weather the inevitable problems that can arise when you're coordinating countless details.

Nancy Tucker, owner of Coordinators' Corner in Richmond, Virginia, puts it this way: "There are so many skills needed for a wedding consultant, but above all they must be personable. They have the task of first selling the need for a wedding consultant and then selling themselves as the right one for the job."

On the more practical side, it also helps to have a strong business background. While it's not impossible to make a go of a wedding consultant business if you've never balanced a checkbook, previous experience with handling finances (even household budgets) as well as managing day-to-day office details is certainly valuable. After all, you'll be coordinating budgets and overseeing finances for your clients. Plus you'll be taking care of the details of running your own business, which will include taxes, billing, and other financial matters. You may even have to deal with personnel administration at some point in your career. So business experience—or barring that, at least a good head for numbers and details—is very important.

Ernst agrees: "Ideally, if a person is going to be able to grow his company, he or she must have an education in basic business, including management, marketing, and accounting."

"An entrepreneurial spirit is also very important," says Julia Kappel, who runs a successful wedding consultant business in a suburb of Dallas. "You have to be able to identify what's good for the business and what isn't, then make the appropriate moves."

The Consulting Life

There are many challenges in this business, to be sure, but along with these challenges come great rewards. Assuming there's no shotgun involved, you're always

▲

Do You Have the Right Stuff?

Take this short quiz to see if you have what it takes to become a successful wedding consultant:

1. Can you juggle a variety of tasks at various stages of development all at the same time?
   ❏ Yes   ❏ No

2. Are you detail oriented?
   ❏ Yes   ❏ No

3. Are you self-motivated and able to work without direct supervision?
   ❏ Yes   ❏ No

4. Are your calendar and other important papers within reach rather than hopelessly buried under piles of office detritus?
   ❏ Yes   ❏ No

5. Are you disciplined enough to work even when the birds are singing, it's sunny and warm outside, and the house needs painting?
   ❏ Yes   ❏ No

6. Are you comfortable working alone without the benefit of chattering co-workers, coffee klatches, and holiday parties?
   ❏ Yes   ❏ No

7. Can you handle emotionally fragile brides, demanding mothers, and irritable suppliers without succumbing to the urge to deck them?
   ❏ Yes   ❏ No

8. Can you say "no" and mean it?
   ❏ Yes   ❏ No

9. Can you laugh unconcernedly when things go wrong, then think fast on your feet to fix them?
   ❏ Yes   ❏ No

10. Can you lead a conga line and do the Cha Cha Slide to get the party started?
    ❏ Yes   ❏ No

Add up your "yes" answers. Scoring:

8 to 10 = Congratulations! You have the makings of an excellent wedding consultant.

4 to 7 = With some hard work, you can go a long way in this field.

1 to 3 = Thank goodness you bought this book.

0 = Maybe you should try a career in trucking or construction!

working with happy (though understandably nervous) people. You're the catalyst that makes the biggest moment of their lives special and memorable. And you can have the satisfaction of seeing all the details you have so painstakingly planned come together seamlessly and effectively.

"The result is definitely the best part," says Crouch. "All I do is eat, sleep, and dream weddings, but it's worth it because it's so much fun."

In addition to the satisfaction of being able to make dream weddings come true for your clients, there's another really appealing reason for embarking on a career in wedding consulting: You become the proud CEO of your own small business. As such, you answer to no one, except maybe the IRS. You can do things your own way. You can set up shop in a spare bedroom or opt for a commercial space. You can set your own hours and make your own schedule. You can take on as much or as little work as you wish. Not that you'll have lots of free time for lazy days on the beach in Maui or strolls down the Champs Elysées. Wedding consulting is hard work. You'll have a mind-boggling number of details to coordinate, oodles of suppliers to baby-sit, long days shifting from one achy foot to the other, and legions of anxious brides (not to mention their mothers) to reassure and soothe.

Does this sound like fun to you, too? Great! Then you've come to the right place. The guide you're holding in your hands will show you how to start a wedding consulting business. It covers day-to-day responsibilities and the various tasks integral to running this type of business. It also touches on the myriad issues a new business owner will confront, such as self-employment taxes, insurance, and financial matters. But perhaps best of all, you'll find that this guide is punctuated with advice and words of wisdom from successful wedding consultants who have turned their personal dreams of working in an industry they love into reality. You can do it, too! So turn the page, and let's get started making your own dreams of self-employment come true.

Here Comes the Wedding Consultant

For pomp, circumstance, and sheer drama, there are few events in life that equal that of a carefully planned wedding. From the solemn ceremony to an elegant country club reception, dresses with yards and yards of pristine white peau de soie and tulle, debonair tuxedoes, and sleek stretch limousines, weddings are as much a staged production as the most elaborate Broadway

Beware!
Avoid conducting casual consultations at your kitchen table or in your basement rec room. If you're going to see clients at home, usher them into a tidy, well-appointed office to reinforce your image as a competent professional.

show. Even if the nuptials are more intimate and the budget more modest, weddings still require a great deal of advanced planning and follow-up to make sure every element of this momentous day comes together as planned—on time and within budget.

In the past, wedding planning activities were often relegated to the mother of the bride or another female family member who had an eye for fashion and a flair for floral design. There was a strict code of appropriate behavior and proper etiquette that dictated exactly how the bridal party should dress and interact.

All has changed with the influx of women into the workplace over the past 30 years. Today's mother of the bride is probably a working woman herself who doesn't have any more time to attend to details such as limousine rentals or reception hall contracts than the bride herself. This has opened a world of opportunity for well-organized, enthusiastic consultants. Professional wedding consultants treat their vocation as a business, not as a pleasant hobby or sideline.

"Today's consultants are men and women trained in the administrative and legal affairs of their industry," says Robbi Ernst III, founder and president of June Wedding Inc. "They are the team leaders who orchestrate the entire wedding, including the wedding day itself."

The Consultant's Role

Toward that end, many wedding consultants routinely serve as event planners, budget watchdogs, etiquette experts, troubleshooters, and on-site supervisors. They accompany brides-to-be to appointments for fittings, floral consultations, and other services. They provide a shoulder to cry on and a sympathetic ear for stressed-out clients. They also act as creative problem-solvers who can quickly assess a situation and devise a viable solution—often without anyone in the bridal party ever knowing a potential disaster has been averted.

Some wedding consultants prefer to offer consulting services only and may provide a comprehensive "wedding blueprint" package that consists of realistic budgets, detailed schedules, and lists of reliable vendors. Still others provide insight and assistance with the social etiquette part of the wedding experience.

Words from the Wise

Robbi Ernst offers these sage words of advice to anyone contemplating a career as a wedding consultant:

○ Seek out the best and most competent professional training in the wedding industry. "Go to the experts and let them teach you not to make the mistakes they made. This can save you a small fortune," Ernst says.

○ Take business and computer courses, including classes on marketing, at your local community college.

○ If possible, work for a well-known consultant for a while as an apprentice.

○ Have enough funds to carry you through three years, since it will take that long before you see a profit.

○ Decide whether you are going to do this as a hobby or as a career. "If you don't make this decision early on, you're going to be frustrated and unhappy," Ernst says.

The scope of your own involvement is entirely up to you. The trend in the industry, however, has been toward offering total coordination of the entire blessed event because, as noted earlier, brides and their mothers just don't have time to attend to the mountain of details necessary to pull off the wedding they dream of. That means you must have an in-depth knowledge of every aspect of wedding planning and know how to make all the details mesh smoothly and effectively.

Bridal Business Basics

No matter how you decide to conduct the majority of your business or what your personal management style may be, there are certain tasks common to all wedding

> **Smart Tip** *Tip...*
> Since you're going to spend a great deal of time on the phone every day, telephone headsets for both your landline and cellphone are a must. Not only does it give you hands-free freedom, but it also saves you from the neck strain that comes from cradling the receiver between your head and your shoulder.

▲

consultants. Among them are day-to-day business administration, bridal consultations, and vendor and service coordination. Here's a look at each of these activities.

A Day in the Life

Even though no two days tend to be alike for wedding consultants because the tastes and needs of their clients vary so widely, there are certain tasks you can expect to do on a regular basis. To begin with, you'll spend lots of time on the telephone every day, fielding inquiries from interested brides, following up on vendor leads, and checking on the status of wedding preparations. If you employ contract or temporary help during weddings, you'll have to meet with them on a regular basis to provide instructions and go over details. You will also spend a significant amount of time with the brides themselves, either conducting consultations or accompanying them to appointments with suppliers.

Then there is the paperwork. You'll have contracts to review, tax forms to file, and other business-related papers to shuffle. You also will have to keep meticulous records on the choices that your brides make, the status of wedding day plans, and other details. A word of advice: No matter how good your memory is, you should always jot down every appointment and activity. The number of details you will have to attend to as a wedding consultant will be truly mind-boggling, and when you're busy and short of time, it will be too easy for something to fall through the cracks—possibly with disastrous results.

The Consultation

The first step in determining what a bride wants and how much she wants to turn over to you is to schedule a consultation. Some novice consultants choose to offer a no-charge consultation, thinking that enticing brides with a glimpse of the magic that can be created will be enough to snag the business. But Robbi Ernst believes this is a mistake. In his book, *Great Wedding Tips From the Experts* (McGraw-Hill), he says, "A genuinely professional wedding consultant isn't going to talk with [anyone] for free, unless it is simply an introductory meeting to determine if you are a good match for each other."

On the other hand, Ann Nola, director of the Association of Certified Professional Wedding Consultants, does offer free consultations that are more than just a brief meeting. The idea is to do some information-gathering that will help ensure smooth sailing for the wedding consultant as much as the bride. "It is just as important for the wedding consultant to know she can work with the bride," Nola says. "You have to see if the personalities match."

According to Ernst, the fee for a single consultation meeting typically ranges from $175 in smaller communities to as much as $500 in metropolitan areas. Charging a fee will help to cut down on the number of women who are just "shopping around" for services without making a commitment.

During a consultation, it is important to determine exactly how much the bride wants you to do. Sometimes, she will prefer to do much of the groundwork herself (such as selecting a reception hall, ordering the cake and flowers, and auditioning the band or DJ), then will ask you to coordinate all the services and be on site during the reception. Other times, a busy bride will want to turn over all or many of these tasks to you, limiting her involvement to approving the choices presented to her and signing checks for the deposits.

For this reason, it's advisable to offer a variety of packages with varying levels of service. The idea is to provide choices that will allow the bride to customize her wedding to her exact specifications.

Suggested wedding packages might include:

- Full-service professional wedding coordination: wedding planning and event supervision from beginning to end
- Rehearsal and wedding day coordination: on-site coordination and execution
- Wedding day-only coordination: full or half-day supervision of wedding party festivities and vendor services
- Pre-wedding consulting package: a wedding blueprint for the DIY brides that includes sample budgets, ready-to-use spreadsheets, detailed schedules, vendor recommendations, and other information
- Party package: planning and coordination of the engagement party, rehearsal dinner, and bachelor and bachelorette parties

Stat Fact
According to the Association for Wedding Professionals International, Las Vegas is the wedding capital of the world, with 106,000 weddings a year, followed by Istanbul, Turkey, with 92,000 weddings annually, and Gatlinburg, Tennessee, with 42,000 nuptials. In fact, Gatlinburg, which is tucked into the heart of the romantic Smoky Mountains, is renowned for its southern hospitality and special wedding packages.

It's common for couples to initially choose the wedding day-only package because they're on a budget or they don't quite grasp the magnitude of the tasks that lie ahead. But eventually, Nola says, they'll find themselves overwhelmed by the planning process and will contact you to request additional services.

Wedding Day Duties

Wedding consultants act as the bride's advocate on the happy day—running interference with suppliers, making sure the wedding party is dressed and where they're supposed to be on time, and so on. But the best consultants go beyond the obvious to make a couple's day special. For example, both Julia Kappel in Oak Point, Texas, and Packy Boukis in Broadview Heights, Ohio, prepare snacks and drinks for the wedding party to nibble on before the wedding so they don't march down the aisle with rumbling stomachs.

To make sure every wedding task runs like clockwork, wedding planners typically create a detailed wedding day schedule that's provided to each member of the wedding party, the parents, and other relatives, as well as to the vendors who are responsible for providing various services. There are software packages that are especially designed to help wedding consultants stay organized and on budget. They're discussed in Chapter 6, "Tools and Equipment that Make Dreams Come True."

Finally, wedding planners often hire extra help on a contract basis to assist with wedding day activities. Typically they handle duties like greeting guests, assisting the wedding party and families (refilling drinks, assisting the bride in the powder room, and so on), and running errands for the wedding planner. Such contractors are hired on an as-needed basis and are paid either by the hour (around $10 to $15 per hour) or by the function ($100 to $150 per day).

Beware!
It's unethical to accept "commissions"—aka kickbacks or referral fees—from the vendors with whom you contract for products or services. This fairly common practice hurts the reputation of the wedding industry, and organizations like the Association of Bridal Consultants strongly discourage accepting such payments, even if you intend to pass the discount on to the bridal couple.

Consulting Services and Fees

Charges for consulting services vary widely. Typically, consultants charge by the package, but some charge by the hour. Others charge 10 to 20 percent of the total wedding cost, but this is a more common practice in larger cities where disposable income is higher and there are more top-level female executives footing the bill.

According to the Association of Bridal Consultants, preparation-planning fees, which include everything except wedding day coordination, averages about $1,500, while pre-wedding guidance (without actual execution of plans) and wedding day coordination typically costs around $3,700. Full production coordination, which includes everything from early planning and budgeting to wedding day coordination, starts at $5,000 but could go much higher depending on the experience of the consultant.

According to the wedding consultants interviewed for this book, full production package rates range from $2,000 to $5,000. The higher prices were found in the largest metropolitan areas, where one consultant even offers a $10,000 "concierge" package for the bride who wants to do nothing more than verbally approve the consultant's selections and hand over a debit card to pay the suppliers.

To arrive at a price for your wedding packages, Gerard J. Monaghan of the Association of Bridal Consultants suggests using this formula to come up with an hourly rate:

$$\text{Dollar amount you want to net annually} \div 50 \text{ weeks}$$
$$\div 5 \text{ days per week} \times 2.5 \text{ (factor for}$$
$$\text{expenses)} = \text{per diem} \div 8 \text{ hours} =$$
$$\text{hourly rate}$$

According to http://weddingplannersalary.org, experienced full-time wedding planners average $75,000 to $90,000 per year, while part-time consultants earn $40,000 to $60,000. But that's in a perfect world—a first-year consultant, who coordinates 10 weddings a year, is more likely to come in at around $24,000 a year, according to Robbi Ernst of June Weddings Inc. Still, you could do better, especially since how much you can charge depends on what your local market will bear.

Stat Fact

Coordinating 10 weddings a year is a good goal to aspire to during the first year of operation, says Gerard J. Monaghan of the Association of Bridal Consultants. An experienced consultant usually can handle about 30 to 40 nuptials per year.

Strategic Market Research

There comes a time in the development of a new business when every prospective business owner gets real about his or her prospects. That point is when the new business owner starts thinking about doing some targeted market research.

Market research will help you lay the groundwork for creating a viable and successful business. It will help you to identify

Stat Fact

The average amount spent on a wedding in 2010, excluding the honeymoon, was $26,984, according to the 2010 Real Weddings Survey of 19,000 U.S. couples. New York City had the highest average wedding budget at $70,730, while Utah had the lowest budget at $13,214.

exactly who might be interested in using your services and whether the area where you want to set up shop can actually sustain your bridal business. Market research also will provide you with useful information and data that can help you avoid operational problems down the road.

Now, you might be thinking, "Hellllo! I'm an aspiring wedding planner, not a statistician. Besides, people get married everywhere. There's bound to be enough business in my area to keep me busy."

Maybe, maybe not. The wedding industry may generate annual retail sales of nearly $71 billion annually, but not every part of the country has the same need for consultants. Take, for instance, those parts of Florida that are heavily populated by senior citizens. It's a safe bet that the chances of making a go at running a successful wedding consultant business in those areas are probably slim to none. Likewise, in rough-and-tumble states like Alaska or Montana, where new jeans are considered formalwear, there is probably a maximum number of consultants the economy can support—or, for that matter, a limited number of people who might actually marry, given the sparse population.

You have to think this way if you want to be successful, and the only way you're going to find out about these kinds of shortcomings—as well as the potential opportunities—is by researching your target market. Fortunately, this is something you can undertake yourself, even if you don't have a background in statistics or research, says David L. Williams, Ph.D., dean of the School of Business at Wayne State University in Detroit.

"With the exception of questionnaire development, which can be difficult for a beginner to do well, you can pretty much handle all of the research by yourself on a reasonably small budget," Williams says. "The problem is, many small-business owners view market research as an optional expense. But it's the only accurate way you have to find out what's important to your customer."

This chapter will show you how to find out who will use your services, learn where they live and work, and determine the kinds of services they'll want you to provide. Armed with this information, you'll be able to make informed decisions that can help your business grow and prosper.

Defining Your Audience

As the song says, "Love makes the world go 'round,'" which means there should be plenty of people who will need your services, right? In theory, yes. But you'll be much more successful if you study the demographics of the area you wish to do business in, then tailor your services to a specific group within that market.

Demographics are defined as the characteristics of the people in your target audience that make them more likely to use your services or products. These characteristics may include age, education, income level, gender, type of residence, and geographic location.

Probably the most significant demographic for wedding consultants to consider is age. According to the U.S. Census Bureau's "2010 Current Population Survey," the average age of today's bride is 26.1, while the average age of the groom is 28.2. So while you certainly can serve people of any age group, you'll probably have the best success and garner the most business if you target brides in their mid-to-late 20s. This also means that if the population base in the area where you wish to do business doesn't have brides in this age group, you must either reconsider your market or adjust your marketing strategy.

Case in point: Brides may be the ultimate consumer for your services, but who sometimes foots the bills for those dream weddings? Mom and Dad, of course, especially since many Gen Xers and Nexters have returned to the nest because of the generally weak economy over the past decade. According to the American Wedding Study, 27 percent of weddings are paid for by the bride's parents, and another 7 percent by both sets of parents. So a viable way to adjust your strategy if you aren't based where the late 20s consumers live is to target their parents instead. That's what Julia Kappel, a suburban Dallas wedding planner, did when her market research showed that the communities around her were populated by couples who were longtime residents and were likely to have children of marriageable age. As a result, she concentrated her advertising efforts in those communities to line up new clients.

Fun Fact

As recently as 30 years ago only the wealthy and socially elite used wedding consultants to coordinate their nuptials. Mothers of the bride generally undertook the complicated task of organizing every aspects of their daughter's wedding.

▲

This is not to say there's no market for your services among older brides. According to statistics from the Center for Disease Control and Prevention/National Center for Health Statistics, of all divorced people aged 25 and older, 44 percent of women and 55 percent of men remarry. These brides are usually older (early 30s and up) and also are prime candidates for your services given the demands of their careers—and their children.

Yet another factor to consider is where your prospective clients live versus where they work. Kappel says brides may look for information, use bridal registries, or purchase their invitations in the area where they work, but they'll go home to get married. That means the wedding consultant may have to travel if he or she wishes to serve the brides who work in the local business community.

Targeting Professional Women

One demographic segment that many wedding consultants serve successfully is that of professional women. These corporate executives or business owners often hold advanced college degrees and have high incomes. Because they don't have time to plan their own weddings, they're more likely to favor full-service packages that make it possible for them to turn all the details over to an experienced planner. Since full-service packages are usually a consultant's highest priced offering, this can translate into significant profits.

Marsha Ballard French and Jenny Cline, wedding consultants based in Dallas, found their niche by targeting professional women. Originally, they intended to coordinate high-profile and celebrity weddings, but found the market was very difficult to break into. By refocusing their efforts on serving professional women instead, the weddings they book now average $30,000.

Packy Boukis, the wedding consultant in Broadview Heights, Ohio, has also successfully captured the professional women's market. She usually communicates with her executive-level brides solely by email and has coordinated every detail of some of her most elaborate and lavish weddings this way.

Stat Fact
The top five most affordable destination wedding spots are Mexico, Las Vegas, Florida, Jamaica, and the Dominican Republic, according to www.weddingsolutions.com, a destination wedding planning site.

Economic Environment

Before we move on, there's one more very important factor to consider in your market research efforts: the economic base in your prospective market area.

Obviously, a wedding consultant is not an absolute necessity when it comes to coordinating a wedding. People get married all the time without ever using consultants' services. What you offer is experience, convenience, and the ability to step in when the details become too time-consuming or overwhelming for a busy bride to manage. So your task not only becomes making your services irresistible to brides, but making sure the people who will pay the bills are financially able to afford your services.

If you've done your market research right, you already have some idea of the average income levels in your neighborhood. Now you need to look at data like the percentage of people who are employed full time and the types of jobs they hold. If the local market is driven by blue-collar, heavy industry jobs, a downturn in the economy could make cash tight and affect your ability to book weddings. So could a plant shutdown or a scaling back of services. A call to your city's economic development office is an easy way to get a handle on the health of local industry in your area.

While you're at it, ask about the area's white-collar jobs and the types of companies that support them. One industry to be wary of is the high-tech industry. Jobs in the information technology sectors are still red hot, but you only have to glance at the Dow Jones industrial averages to know that tech stocks experience huge swings in both directions. So again, an economy that's based on high-tech jobs has the potential to go south, taking your prospective customers with it. You need to make sure you have

Destination Romance

Richard Markel, of the Association for Wedding Professionals International, estimates that at least 12 percent of weddings are destination weddings. The reason? "The internet," he says. "It's given us the capability to find anything anywhere. People have formed tour companies all around the country just to handle destination events like weddings."

The internet also has opened legions of opportunities for wedding consultants who live and work in highly desirable locations such as Orlando (with Disney World), Hawaii (with its slice of paradise), and New York City (with its cosmopolitan flair). Other tropical locales like Tahiti, St. Lucia, and the U.S. Virgin Islands are popular destination weddings sites, while the most affordable destination spots are Mexico, Las Vegas, and Florida. Wedding consultants who are willing to handle the extra challenges involved in coordinating destination weddings may find they're not as restricted by the vagaries of the local economy.

Beware!
Mailing lists are purchased for one-time use. Lists are "seeded" with control names so the seller will know if you use the list more than one time. If you wish to use the list more than once, you'll have to ante up again.

a backup survival plan if you aspire to serve an area that's heavily dependent on a single industry.

Conducting Market Research

Now that you have a general idea about the types of people who might be responsive to your marketing efforts, you can proceed to the next step, which is to conduct an organized market research study. Your goal is to touch base with potential customers to find out whether they'd be interested in using the services of a wedding consultant, as well as exactly what types of services they may require.

There are two kinds of research: primary, which is information gathered firsthand; and secondary, which is information culled from external sources. Each has its own merits as well as costs.

Primary Research

The most common forms of primary research used by wedding consultants are direct mail surveys, telemarketing campaigns, and personal interviews. Assuming that you'll want to save your startup capital for equipment and advertising, you should probably try a survey first since it's the most cost-effective way to gather information. By the same token, you might try doing the survey yourself rather than hiring a market research firm because that can be quite expensive.

Your survey should be no more than a page long, since it's difficult to get busy people to fill out anything lengthier. The questions should be well-phrased so they're direct, clear, and unambiguous. They also should be constructed so the information they gather is conducive to analysis. For example, a question like "Would you be interested in hiring a wedding consultant?" isn't very useful because it's closed-ended, meaning it's possible for the respondent to give a "yes" or "no" answer without elaborating. That's not going to give you much insight, which is the whole point of this exercise.

Although you can certainly draft the questions yourself, you should consider asking someone experienced in market research for help. Since a market research firm tends to be pricey, Williams, dean of the Wayne State University School of Business,

Stat Fact

According to Richard Markel of the Association for Wedding Professionals International, at any given time, just under 1 percent of the population is planning a wedding. The trick is to find that group within your geographic area and target your marketing efforts toward them.

suggests contacting the business school at your local university instead. A marketing professor on staff might be willing to draft your questionnaire for $500 to $1,000, or may even assign your questionnaire as a class project, as Williams himself has done. In the meantime, you'll find a sample market research questionnaire on pages 25 and 25 that you can use as a guideline.

Surveying the Market

This part is easier than you might think. Start by purchasing a mailing list that's targeted to the market you wish to reach. Local trade associations, list brokers, and even daily newspapers in major metropolitan areas can sell you a list of heads of households that can be sorted in many ways, including by ZIP code, so you can target a specific geographic area. You can find a huge listing of publications that sell their lists in the Standard Rate and Data Service Directory (published by VNU), which you should be able to access for free at your local library. Some other criteria you are bound to be interested in will include occupation (if you are looking for professional women), gender (since women are the primary consumers of bridal consulting services), and age (as in 30-ish or the parental age brackets). Need another list source? Try the Directory of U.S. Associations (published by Consumer Marketing Group), which can be found at most large libraries. You also can sign up for a free trial at www.marketingsource.com.

Once you have your list in hand (which is usually priced as a flat rate per 1,000 names), you're ready to produce your questionnaire. To keep the cost down, format it yourself on a home computer, then bop over to a quick print shop like Kinko's or Staples and have copies run off on your company letterhead.

Reel 'Em In

How would you like an easy way to improve your response rates? Try enclosing a crisp, new dollar bill with your survey. The dollar is sent as a thank you to the recipient for taking the time to fill out and return the questionnaire. Although it does not

Smart Tip

Tip...

Privileged Insights, an online boutique marketing group, offers a free market research report and a monthly wedding marketing newsletter specifically for bridal industry specialists. Sign up at www.privilegedinsights.com.

Market Research Questionnaire

Special Occasions Bridal Consulting

1010 Park Avenue
Lincoln Park, Michigan 10101

June 13, 20xx

Ms. Susan Pfeiffer
10 Spring Lake Road
Bloomfield Hills, Michigan 10101

Dear Ms. Pfeiffer:

Congratulations on your recent engagement! This is an exciting time in your life, and I wish you much happiness.

I am about to start a wedding consulting business in Oakland County that will assist happy brides-to-be like you with the many details necessary to organize a picture-perfect wedding. Would you please take a few minutes to answer the following questions so I can assist brides better?

What is your age?

❏ 18–24 ❏ 35–39
❏ 25–29 ❏ 40–44
❏ 30–34 ❏ 45 and up

Which of the following services might interest you as you plan your wedding? (Check all that apply.)

❏ Assistance with setting up and staying within budget

❏ Information about reliable vendors (i.e., florists, caterers, bakers, etc.)

❏ Assistance with selecting and meeting with vendors

❏ Assistance with planning your entire wedding

❏ Services of a wedding consultant on the wedding day

Market Research Questionnaire, continued

❑ Coordination of the rehearsal dinner

❑ Handling of honeymoon arrangements

Have you ever considered using a wedding consultant?

❑ Yes   ❑ No

Would you prefer to pay a flat fee or a percentage of your wedding costs for wedding consultant services?

❑ Flat fee   ❑ Percentage

If you hired a consultant who charged a flat fee, how much would you be willing to pay?

❑ $1,000–$1,500

❑ $1,501–$2,000

❑ $2,001–$2,500

❑ more than $2,500, depending on the complexity of the wedding

What is your household income?

❑ $25,000–$50,000   ❑ $50,001–$75,000   ❑ $75,000 and up

What is your educational level?

❑ High school diploma   ❑ College degree

❑ Graduate school degree   ❑ Doctorate degree

What is your profession?

_____

_____

If you would like to be contacted by a wedding consultant, provide your phone number or email address here:

( ) _____

email: _____

guarantee a response and doesn't buy much these days, the buck certainly is an attention-getter, and direct marketing studies have shown that sending even such a small cash honorarium does tend to improve the rate of return.

Of course, this trick could cost you a pretty penny, so to speak, since Williams says that surveys should be sent to a sample of at least 300 people to get useful data. However, even as few as 100 surveys would be useful and would only require a $100 investment if you choose to include a monetary incentive.

Smart Tip

Tip...

Compiled lists are lists of names that have been culled from published sources such as organization rosters, conference attendees, and utility companies. Hot lists include contact information for known buyers and are usually taken from magazine subscription lists, mail order buyer lists, and so on. Hot lists cost more to rent because the information is usually fresher and more accurate.

Phone It In

Since you probably love people and already have strong people skills if you're planning to get into a service industry like wedding consulting, telemarketing is a natural, if time-consuming, way to gather information. As with surveys, you'll need a strong telemarketing script with questions similar to those on your market research questionnaire and a good prospect list. But when you call, don't just fill out the form. Listen carefully to the person on the other end of the line. She's bound to make comments and have concerns about things you've never even considered. That helps you add to the storehouse of knowledge you'll tap into when you're ready to go after your first client.

Beware!

Prospect lists purchased from list brokers should be clean and vetted against the national Do Not Call list. But if you happen to call someone who wasn't weeded out by the list broker, apologize and hang up. Then report the name and phone number to the list broker so the individual isn't bothered again.

A Job for the Pros

If you're really nervous about doing your own market research and have a sufficiently large startup budget, you could engage a market research firm to help you. These firms are located in most large cities and will be listed in the Yellow Pages or online. They will not only collect information for you, but they'll also handle all incoming data, then analyze the results and prepare a report for your review.

Williams says a smaller firm might charge you $2,000 to $3,000 to handle a mailed or emailed survey project and prepare a simple report. The cost for 200 to 300 interviews and a report would be about $4,000 to $8,000.

Finally, keep abreast of what's happening in your target market area by reading the local newspaper and listening to or watching the local news. Media outlets usually track trends that affect their broadcast area, and it's easy to visit their websites to obtain the 411. You also can visit the websites of local government entities at the city, township, and county/borough/parish level. Look for a link to economic development information to find demographics and other useful information you can put to good use in your marketing plan.

Secondary Research

If you're looking for real cost savings when doing market research, try using secondary research. Someone, somewhere has probably researched something that relates to what you want to know, and you can often put your hands on that information free of charge.

The mother lode of statistical information can be found at state and federal agencies, since they collect data on everything from income levels to buying habits. Although this data may be a year or two old, it can still be very useful, particularly for the fledgling wedding consultant who does not have much money to spend on research. Some great sources of information are the U.S. Census Bureau (www.census. gov), the SBA (www.sba.gov), local economic development organizations, and even utility companies, which often have demographic data they will provide free of charge or for a very nominal fee.

Other sources of useful secondary research include your local library and chamber of commerce, your state's economic development department, trade associations, and trade publications. You can find the names of thousands of trade publications in the Standard Rate and Data Service Directory (published by VNU). And, of course, the internet is an invaluable source of just about any information you require. Just be sure to gather information only from reputable sites, such as organizations with good business reputations or those that appear to have rock solid data sources themselves.

Dollar Stretcher

The SBA offers a wealth of free information on how to write a marketing plan, as well as insight on many other issues related to small-business development. You'll find the 411 at www.sba.gov. Also try typing "free marketing plan templates" into your browser and see what pops up.

Writing a
Mission Statement

Understanding your market and the people you'll serve is critical to the success of your business. But understanding yourself and defining exactly what you plan to do as a wedding consultant is equally important. So follow the lead of America's most successful corporations and write a simple mission statement that includes your company's goals and outlines how you will fulfill them.

What might a typical mission statement for a wedding consulting business say? Here are a couple of examples:

> *Bride's Choice will serve the needs of busy professional women by providing a full range of wedding consultation services. Thanks to my prior hands-on experience with wedding planning for several friends and family members, I am confident I will be able to coordinate 10 weddings in my first year of operation.*

Here's another possible approach to a mission statement:

> *Hearts and Flowers Inc. is poised to become the premier wedding consultant service in greater Ashtabula. With our network of reliable suppliers, our personal background in business management, and our extensive network of social and business contacts, we bring an extra measure of experience to the business that will inspire confidence in our clients. Our goal is to achieve sales of $50,000 in calendar year 2012–2013.*

Your mission statement is your compass as well as the foundation on which your business's future is built. It can be one sentence long, as in the case of Pepsi's mission statement—whose succinct version is "Beat Coke"—or it can be several paragraphs. The length doesn't matter; the direction it provides is what's important. We've provided a worksheet on the next page to get you thinking about what you want to include in the mission statement for your business.

Mission Statement Worksheet

Here's your opportunity to try your hand at writing your own mission statement. Start out by answering the following questions:

1. What are your reasons for becoming a wedding consultant?

   _____

   _____

2. What are your personal objectives? How do you intend to achieve them?

   _____

   _____

3. What skills do you bring to the business that will be of benefit?

   _____

   _____

4. What is your vision for this business? Where do you think you can take it in one, two, and five years?

   _____

   _____

   _____

Using this information, write your mission statement here:

Mission Statement for

_____
(your company name)

_____

_____

_____

_____

Business Basics

Just as a bridal gown has a couture "superstructure" made of satin overlays, lace insets, and rustling tulle, a wedding consulting business needs a formal framework to ensure compliance with commonly accepted business practices. This chapter delves into standard operating procedures for everything

▲

Dollar Stretcher

Use the internet to do your own initial business name search for free. First, check for trademarks registered nationally on the U.S. Patent and Trademark Office website at www.uspto.gov. Then go to the corporation and business name website in your state to find out whether the name you've chosen is available.

from legal matters to business insurance and shows you how to get your business machine oiled, cranked up, and ready to run.

It's All in a Name

Choosing a name for your company should be high on your list of priorities in the early stages of business development. Many wedding consultants use their own names combined with a business description, like "Eileen Figure Bridal Consulting." But Robbi Ernst III, president and founder of June Wedding Inc., believes that's not a good idea.

"Someday you may want to retire or otherwise leave the business and do something else, and you'll want to sell the company," he says. "The very real problem with using a personal name for the company is that unless the person who buys a company named 'Weddings by Lara' is named Lara, too, she'll have to change the name. This is a problem because through the years of its life, a company builds a reputation for integrity, quality, professionalism, and creativity based on that name. That reputation has monetary value and is part of what a buyer is purchasing."

Still, you certainly can incorporate your own name in the business name if that's what you really want. And of course, you should select a simple, businesslike name that identifies who you are without being too cute. That means staying away from names that are too over-the-top, like "Smart Broads Wedding Services," "Hugs and Kisses Weddings," or "Your First Wedding." Not only are these types of names not professional, but they won't inspire confidence in your clientele.

Lisa Kronauer, a Connecticut-based wedding consultant, is one business owner who eschewed her own name in favor of one with a touch of sophistication. She selected "Studio K" because it could encompass all areas of her business, from wedding planning to general event planning.

Smart Tip

Tip...

If you are coordinating weddings in a part of the country that has a large ethnic population, consider how your name might translate into other languages. English is highly dependent on metaphors, and that lovely name you've chosen may translate into something incomprehensible in another language.

Another of the wedding consultants interviewed for this book chose her romantic-sounding name, "Ever After Weddings," specifically because she didn't want her own name in the title.

"It seems to me that these are not ever my weddings and by using a name like 'Weddings by Lisa,' it implies control," says Lisa Michael, a wedding consultant in Montana. "That's a myth [about wedding consulting] that I wanted to discredit, not encourage."

There can be other compelling reasons for a name choice. Dolores Enos, a wedding consultant in Larkspur, California, started her business in 1991 under one name. In 1999 she took a well-deserved sabbatical, then decided to reopen the business under a new name that started with the letter "A." The reason, she says: "I'm now first in the phone book."

Not everyone can be listed in that coveted first spot, but you can choose a unique name that's distinctive and evocative of what your business does. To help you get started, check the Yellow Pages or the internet for ideas (as well as to avoid duplication). Or you can do what Loreen Crouch, a wedding consultant in Ypsilanti, Michigan, did before settling on a business name. After polling her friends, she came up with a list of about 50 names, which she narrowed down to 10 finalists. Then she put those names to a vote before deciding on "Design My Wedding." She knew she made the right choice when she was in the post office one day and a woman who saw her carrying a box with her return address asked if she planned weddings.

Everyone Can Have a June Wedding

Wedding consultants frequently invest a great deal of time and thought into selecting a name for their business—and with good reason. It's a big responsibility selecting a name that's clever and evocative, yet accurately describes what you do and is something you can live with for a long time.

Robbie Ernst, founder and president of June Wedding, says he had a lot of fun selecting the name for his company. "We purposefully chose the month of June for our name since this is popular jargon in wedding industry talk. But it also was purely a marketing ploy that we chose the singular 'June Wedding' as opposed to the plural 'June Weddings.' The intent was to suggest that everyone can have a June wedding, even if she gets married during a snowy winter or during the sweltering humidity of August."

"You need a name that catches the eye and provides instant recognition of what you do," Crouch stresses. "That day in the post office proved that my business name did both."

You'll find a worksheet on pages 35 and 36 that you can use to help you select an appropriate moniker. Once you have picked a suitable name, it's time to move on to the next step: setting up your business structure.

Registering Your Company Name

Most states require you to register your fictitious company name officially to ensure that it's unique. This is usually done at the county level and is known as filing a dba ("doing business as") statement. (You can save yourself the trouble of standing in line at the county courthouse by checking to see if your local jurisdiction offers online filing.) The fee to file is usually nominal (around $10 to $50) and entitles you to use the name for a limited period of time, usually three to five years. When the time expires, you simply renew the dba. Before you get your dba, however, a search is done to make sure your name is unique. If you happen to choose a name that's already being used, you'll have to pick something else, so it's a good idea to have a couple of names in reserve.

Your Corporate Structure

Once you have your dba in hand, you are considered the proud owner of a legitimate business. So naturally, the IRS will have something to say about the way you run it. (You knew we'd get around to the IRS eventually, didn't you?) Basically, this means the bureaucrats in Washington require that you operate as one of four business entities: sole proprietorship, corporation, partnership, or limited liability company (LLC).

Sole Proprietors

Most wedding consultants operate as sole proprietors because it's the easiest and least expense type of business to form. All you have to do is file a dba as discussed above, then open a business checking account in that name. You can use your personal credit

A Name for All Reasons

Establishing a unique business identity is not just important; it's absolutely essential so prospective clients (and, alas, the IRS) can find you easily. Try the following brainstorming exercise to whittle down your choices and find the perfect name.

List the top three things that come to mind when you hear the word "wedding" (such as bride or bouquet). Be creative!

1._____

2._____

3._____

List three unique landmarks or features that characterize the place where you'll do business (such as the sand dunes of northern Michigan or the picturesque caves of Carlsbad).

1._____

2._____

3._____

List three geographical references (such as your city, state, or regional area).

1._____

2._____

3._____

Now, try combining elements from these three sections in different ways:

1._____

2._____

3._____

Did you come up with something you liked? If not, try using alliteration ("Weddings in White") or plays on words ("Altared State") with any of the elements above to create a business name.

Once you've selected a name, put it to the test:

○ Say it aloud several times to make sure it's easily understood, both in person and over the phone. A name like "Simply Sensational Celebrations" has too many "s" sounds and may be difficult to pronounce, let alone understand on the phone.

○ Page through your local Yellow Pages directory to make sure someone else isn't already using the name you've chosen.

○ Check with your county seat or other official registrar to make sure the name is available. Someone may have already claimed the name but may not be using it yet.

○ Does your name pass the test? Way to go! Now you're ready to register it officially.

card to pay for business expenditures, yet you still get tax benefits like business expense deductions. But there is a downside to the sole proprietorship. You are personally liable for any losses, bankruptcy claims, legal actions, and so on. That can wipe out both your personal and business assets if a catastrophe hits.

General Partnership

If you are planning to join forces with another wedding consultant to open a business, you are forming a general partnership. Partnerships are easier to form than corporations, and you don't have to file any documents to make them legal. But since each partner is responsible for the actions of the other, it's a good idea to have a partnership agreement drawn up by an attorney. That way, you can spell out exactly what each person is responsible for.

Limited Liability Company

A third type of business entity is the limited liability company, or LLC, which combines the tax structure of a partnership, yet protects the business owner from personal liability. This is the type of partnership agreement Marsha Ballard French and Jenny Cline, the wedding consultants in Dallas, drew up when they started their business. Even though they had known each other for decades and brought complementary skills to the partnership, they recognized how important it was to protect their personal interests.

Corporations

The last type of business arrangement is the corporation. It is established as a legal entity completely separate from the business owner. Establishing a corporation requires filing articles of incorporation, electing officers, and holding an annual meeting. Not many wedding consultants choose this route initially because the costs are prohibitive and the company must pay corporate taxes. On the other hand, a corporation will find it easier to obtain financing, which would be useful if you decided to franchise your business, start a retail store that caters to brides, or expand in a big way.

Ernst recommends that wedding consultants incorporate immediately. "Corporation status is especially important if you have a lot of assets or you have a family you want to protect," he says.

Incidentally, if you operate under your own name, you can use your Social Security number when filing your business taxes. But if you adopt another name for your sole proprietorship, or form a partnership or corporation, you are required to have a federal Employer Identification Number (EIN). To apply for one, go to www.irs.gov and print a copy of form SS-4. Alternatively, you may obtain an EIN immediately by calling the IRS Business & Specialty Tax Line at (800) 829-4933.

Making a Choice

So which legal form is best for your new business? Daniel H. Minkus, a member of the business practice group of Clark Hill PLC, says an attorney can help you decide which entity is best for your situation. "If you don't know the people you are doing business with, I'd encourage you to form a single-member LLC or corporation," Minkus says. "They're simple to create, and they're invaluable because your clients are dealing with your enterprise and not you personally."

According to the website www.legalzoom.com, it can cost $500 to $700 or more to incorporate using an attorney, which includes the cost of filing the required documents. Corporations also must pay an additional $50 to $200 in government filing fees, as well as secretary of state filing fees for your state.

Because there are so many fees, some new business owners choose to go it alone. Generally, you can save hundreds of dollars by filing yourself. But LegalZoom warns that novices often make mistakes when filing on their own that could put their company in jeopardy in a court of law. In addition, corporate law is complex and difficult to understand. So it's usually best to have a professional to handle it for you. You'll find information about hiring an attorney in Chapter 5, "Getting Professional Help."

> **Fun Fact**
> Homebased businesses make up about half of all U.S. businesses, and more than 90 percent of those homebased businesses are sole proprietorships, according to the SBA Office of Advocacy.

Setting Up Shop

Just when you thought it was safe to test the waters with your new business, you find out there could be a restriction on your activities. That could come in the form of a local zoning ordinance, which prohibits businesses to operate in certain areas like residential neighborhoods. Such ordinances exist to protect people from excessive traffic and noise (as well as to rake in the extra taxes assessed on businesses). But because your business doesn't require signage and you won't have a lot of people coming and going, it's quite likely you can run the business quietly from your home. Still, to be on the safe side, you should check with your local government office to see if any special permits are required. It's better to find out upfront, before you go to the expense of printing stationery and obtaining a business telephone line, than to find out later that homebased businesses are prohibited in your area.

It's especially important to check local zoning regulations if you plan to do consultations with prospective clients in your home. You may need to establish a business office elsewhere, as Julia Kappel, the wedding consultant in Oak Point, Texas, did when she rented a 1,500-square-foot townhouse and converted it into a business office separate from her home.

> **Beware!**
> Zoning regulations are established at the local (city, township, or village) level rather than the state level. A homebased business that's perfectly legal in one city could be verboten in another. The only way to find out is by calling the zoning board in your community.

Other Licenses and Permits

But wait, there's more! Some municipalities require business owners to have a business license. It's usually available for a very nominal fee and is renewable annually. If by chance you are turned down for a license because of zoning restrictions, you can apply for (and probably receive) a variance from the municipal planning commission so you can get your license.

Then there's the health department permit that would be necessary from the county where you do business if you provide any of the food at your weddings. A permit is also necessary if you bake the wedding cake yourself, says Donna Horner, an Austin, Texas, consultant. An experienced baker who started out in the wedding industry by baking cakes for military personnel on a local military base, Horner doesn't trust the job to anyone else. So she dutifully renews her health certificate every year so she can continue her personal tradition of baking for her brides.

To find out whether you need other special permits or licenses, you can contact:

- SBA. See the federal listings in your phone book, or go to www.sba.gov.
- Small Business Development Center (SBDC). Find your local office through the SBA, or by logging onto www.sba.gov.
- SCORE. This nonprofit organization is an SBA partner and has hundreds of chapters throughout the United States. Its members can advise you on permit requirements and much more, all at no charge. Go to www.score.org.

Writing a Business Plan

There's still one more task you have to complete before you can leave this chapter and plunge into the other uncharted waters that await you. And this is a big one—one that literally can make or break your business.

You have to write a scintillating, compelling, and painfully comprehensive business plan that will guide you through the aforementioned Bermuda Triangle of Business.

Your business plan is like GPS for your business. It outlines your plans, goals, and strategies for making your business successful. It's useful not just for applying for credit or attracting investors, but it also gives

Smart Tip

Tip...

Experts say that a thoroughly researched business plan should be about 25 pages long and takes 300 hours to prepare (which includes doing research, compiling financial information, conducting surveys, and writing). This may seem like a lot of work, but a plan that's too sketchy will neither keep you on the right course nor help you find financing, if needed.

you direction so you can achieve even your loftiest goals as well as measure the success of your business over time.

There are seven major components a business plan should have. Here's how they apply to a bridal consulting business:

1. *Executive summary.* In this section, which summarizes the entire business plan, you'll describe the nature of your business, the scope of the services you offer (including brief details about the various wedding packages you'll offer, additional services like retail goods sales and so on), the legal form of operation (discussed earlier in this chapter), and your goals. If you plan to use the business plan to seek financing for your company, you should include details about your future plans for the business, too.

2. *Business description.* In this section, you'll want to describe both the bridal industry and your target market. (You'll find general statistics about the bridal industry in the guide you're holding.) This is a good place to include your mission statement, as well as a discussion of your company goals and objectives.

3. *Market strategies.* Here's another place where all that market research data will come in handy. In this section, you'll want to analyze exactly what you'll do to reach prospective brides and how you'll pull it off. Focus, too, on the things that make your company unique, from your personal experience in event planning to specialized business know-how or other factors. Refer back to Chapter 3, "Strategic Market Research," for information about marketing plans.

4. *Competitive analysis.* If you have done your homework well, you already know how many wedding consultants are in business in your target market area. But in this section, you should also consider other potential competitors, such as general event planners who also coordinate weddings and banquet facilities that offer consulting services. Analyze their strengths and weaknesses, and contrast them against what you perceive to be your own strengths. Also, don't forget to consider the aspects that make your services unique and special.

5. *Design and development plan.* Here's where you'll consider how you will develop market opportunities to help your company prosper and grow. It's

> **Smart Tip**
>
> The SBA offers several free courses to help entrepreneurs realize their dream of business ownership, including one called "How to Prepare a Business Plan." The self-paced online courses take about 30 minutes to complete. Go to www.sba.gov/content/online-courses-starting-your-business to get going.

helpful to create a timetable of objectives that you can refer to as benchmarks for your successes, like setting a goal for graduating from 10 weddings a year to 20 and how much contract help you'll need to accomplish this.

6. *Operations and management plan.* Use the information in Chapter 2, "Here Comes the Wedding Consultant," which discusses the day-to-day operations of your business, as a guide for drafting this section. You should keep this section of your marketing plan updated to reflect any new or expanded services you offer.

7. *Financial factors.* Even if you're a sole proprietor with very modest first-year expectations, you need to forecast the success of your business. This will help keep your business on track and help you avoid nasty surprises later on. Probably the most important document in this section is your balance sheet, which will provide a running tally of how well your business is doing.

Constructing such a detailed business plan may sound like a lot of nonessential work, especially since you're probably operating out of your den or from your dining room table. But embarking on a new business without a clear-cut plan is like sailing for Europe without a navigational chart or a compass. Without a plan, you won't have any idea to whom you're selling your services or what they're even interested in. So take the time to formalize your business plan now, then refer back to it periodically for both inspiration and direction.

Business Startup Checklist

Be sure to address these essentials when launching your business:

- ❏ Select a business name and apply for a dba.
- ❏ Consult with an attorney regarding the best legal form for your business.
- ❏ Apply for an Employer Identification Number (using Form SS-4) if you're forming a corporation.
- ❏ Check local zoning regulations.
- ❏ Apply for a business license if required in your community.
- ❏ Write your business plan.
- ❏ Contact an accountant to discuss the financial and tax requirements related to establishing and operating your business.

Getting Professional Help

Just as a busy bride will turn over the details of planning her wedding extravaganza to you, so you will want to relinquish some of the details of running your business to other professionals who have the expertise to do the job right. Even if you have the know-how to do your own taxes or review a real estate lease, this isn't necessarily a good use of your time. It's almost always better to spend the lion's share of your working hours on the activity you do best—wedding planning—and rely on other professionals to keep your business humming along behind the scenes. This chapter will give you insight into why you should consider hiring an attorney, an accountant, and an insurance agent, as well as what you can expect them to do for you.

> **Dollar Stretcher**
>
> A prepaid legal plan is a good alternative for small-business owners whose legal needs are modest. Plans cost as little as $10 per month and vary by state, but usually give you access to services like telephone consultations, letter writing, and contract review by a qualified attorney, as well as a discounted rate on other services.

The Legal Eagle

You're reliable and prompt, conscientious, and professional, so you couldn't possibly ever have to worry about being sued by one of your sweet, blushing brides, or the members of her family, right?

Wrong. Unfortunately, whenever a job involves working with the public, the potential to be sued exists. The lawsuit could be over a matter that you couldn't possibly have controlled, like a sudden torrential downpour that flooded the streets and trapped the caterer in her car on a low-lying street so the mostaccioli didn't arrive until after the guests did. Or it could be over something more unthinkable, such as having one of your contract workers show up tipsy and unruly, and fall face-first into the cake.

So it makes sense to retain an attorney before anything ever goes wrong so you have someone to turn to for advice and guidance when the time comes. The main reasons a wedding consultant might have for hiring an attorney include:

- Wanting to form a partnership or a corporation
- Finding the language in a contract difficult to understand
- Signing a contract for a large sum of money or one that will cover a long period of time (such as a long-term lease on an office site)
- Being sued or having someone threatening to sue
- Needing help with tax planning, loan negotiations, or employee contracts

"But above all, protecting yourself from liability is one of the most important things you must do as a small-business owner," says Daniel H. Minkus, a member of the business practice group of Clark Hill PLC. "An attorney can help you assess your risk for being party to a lawsuit and help you minimize it."

As you know from Chapter 4, "Business Basics," establishing an LLC or a corporation is a good way to limit the liability on your personal property. Limiting your financial liability when hiring an attorney is just as important, especially when you're just starting out and your cash flow is modest. Minkus says that because you don't need a litigator (someone who will defend you in court against lawsuits) to handle your legal work at the outset, you can keep costs down by hiring an attorney in a one- or two-person practice.

Smart Tip

Turn to the internet for help when hiring an attorney. The website www.lawyers.com offers advice on everything from determining when you should seek the sage advice of a lawyer to guiding you through the preparations you'll need to make before meeting with an attorney.

Attorneys' hourly rates typically run from $200 to $600, with the higher rates being charged by senior partners and those who work at larger firms. Other factors that

Choosing the Right Attorney

It's important to find a lawyer who meets your personal needs and expectations, as well as someone whose strong communication skills make him or her easy to talk to. Here are some questions you can ask that can be helpful in determining whether you and your attorney will make a great couple:

- ○ What's your background and experience?
- ○ What's your specialty?
- ○ How long have you been practicing?
- ○ Do you have other consultants or small-business owners as clients?
- ○ Have you ever represented a wedding consultant before?
- ○ Will you do most of the work, or will a paralegal or other aide help out?
- ○ Is there a charge for an initial consultation?
- ○ What do you charge for routine legal work?
- ○ Do you work on a contingency basis?

▲

influence cost include geographic location, the experience of the attorney, and the attorney's area of expertise.

You may be required to pay an initial consultation fee, so it's important to ask about this before you ever set foot in the lawyer's office. In addition, you may have to pay your attorney a retainer upfront, which he or she will draw against as work is completed. Others work on a contingency basis, which means they will take a percentage of any lawsuit settlement that's reached. Still others charge a flat fee for routine work, such as filing incorporation papers.

Another way to keep your legal costs reasonable is simply by being organized. "Do your own legwork to gather the information you need beforehand, then limit the number of office visits you must make," Minkus advises. "You also should limit the number of phone calls you make to your attorney, because you'll be charged for those, too."

Many attorneys offer startup packages that are often more affordable for the small-business owner. While you usually can tailor such packages to meet your needs, they typically include an initial consultation, as well as all activities related to the LLC or incorporation process, including the filing of paperwork with your state and other corporate formalities. You can expect to pay approximately $1,200 to $1,500 to set up a corporation, although as mentioned in Chapter 4, you can save money by using an online legal resource like legalzoom.com. A payment plan may be available to help you handle the cost.

You can incorporate without an attorney by using an incorporation kit or legal service available on the internet. But when establishing something as important as the business that will be your livelihood, it's recommended you seek professional help to launch your professional enterprise. But if you really do want to go it alone, check out a site like www.legalzoom.com, where in addition to paying filing fees, you'll pay $139 to incorporate, or $149 to establish an LLC.

Locating an attorney you like and respect is often as simple as asking friends or relatives for a referral. In any event, Minkus says that process is much more reliable than just going online and picking someone at random. Another way to find a lawyer is through the state bar association in your state, or through online sources like www.findanattorney.us, www.lawyers.com, and the *Martindale-Hubbell Law Directory* at www.martindale.com.

Money Manager

It's usually easier to convince a new business owner that he or she needs an accountant over other business consultants, like attorneys. Most people are either

Smart Tip

Tip...

If you're comfortable doing your own bookkeeping and just need tax help, you could hire an enrolled agent instead of an accountant. In addition to preparing your tax return, enrolled agents can represent you before the IRS. They can be found through the National Association of Enrolled Agents (www.naea.org).

admirably adept or totally clueless when it comes to budgeting, bookkeeping, and other financial matters. But even those who feel comfortable cranking out their personal taxes annually or investing online may blanche at the thought of creating profit and loss statements and other complex documents. That's usually a pretty reliable sign that you need to "book" the services of a professional accountant.

An accountant can help you establish an effective record-keeping system, help you keep expenses in line, and monitor cash flow. He or she also can advise you on tax issues, which is crucial because tax law is very complicated and changes frequently. Tax issues that might be relevant to a wedding consultant include the amount you can deduct annually for business expenses, including travel, entertainment, and office equipment; and the amount of money you can deposit to your Simplified Employee Pension plan (SEP) annually. To learn more about SEPs, see IRS Publication 650, *Retirement Plans for Small Business (SEP, SIMPLE and Qualified Plans)*, or Publication 4333, *SEP Retirement Plans for Small Businesses*. Both are available at www.irs.gov.

Like an attorney, an accountant experienced in handling small-business tax issues can advise you whether you should incorporate your business. In addition to protecting your personal assets, incorporating can cut your tax bill, allow you to put more money into your personal investments, and offer other useful benefits.

There are two types of accountants. Certified public accountants, or CPAs, are college-educated and must pass a rigorous certification examination in the state where they do business to put those coveted letters after their names. Public accountants aren't certified and don't have to be licensed by the state. While they may be perfectly capable due to their experience, they usually can't represent you before the IRS if you're called in for an audit, as CPAs can.

There's also a plethora of accounting software on the market that can help you crunch the numbers and manage your business accounting. Intuit QuickBooks is the choice of many small-business owners because it's thorough and easy to

Bright Idea

A Simplified Employee Pension Plan (SEP) has a higher contribution limit than a traditional IRA (25 percent of the employee's income, or $49,000, whichever is lower), and your funds grow tax-deferred. An accountant or financial planner can help you with the paperwork necessary to set up this important retirement savings plan.

use. However, managing your finances does take time away from your main job—coordinating weddings—so you may want to have a professional handle the more time-consuming activities like tax filings.

According to the Journal of Accountancy, in 2010 the hourly rate charge by an accountant ranged from $117 at the smallest firms to $319 at the largest companies. You can keep the cost of doing business down by dropping out of the School of Shoebox Accounting and organizing your financial records and receipts before you meet with your accountant. You'll find more bookkeeping strategies and techniques in Chapter 12.

To find an accountant, ask your attorney, banker, or other professionals in the wedding industry for a referral. There also are a number of online referral services, including www.CPAfinder.com and www.accountant-finder.com, that can refer you to a qualified number cruncher. It's very important to select someone who has experience either with small-business clients in general or wedding consultants in particular (although this can be a tall order, depending on your area of the country). Avoid accountants who specialize in large corporations, since they may not be as tuned into small-business tax and financial matters as a smaller company may be.

Covering Your Assets

The other business professional you should have on your side is an insurance agent. Although you could use one of the services that guide you to discount insurance brokers via the internet, it's probably better to find an agent in your own community instead (or at least at the time of startup; you can comparison shop and switch later). This will allow you to discuss the particulars of your own business with an agent face-to-face to make sure you're covered against all potential pitfalls. You'll also want an experienced agent who is familiar with the risks you might encounter in your business and can recommend exactly how much coverage you need to protect yourself against those risks.

Start your search for an insurance agent by contacting the person who currently insures your home, apartment, or automobile, or go to his or her company's website, where you're likely to find an agent locator. Another viable option is an independent insurance agent, who sells a variety of insurance products, including life, health, casualty, and other types of insurance that might be of interest to a small-business owner. They may even sell mutual funds and offer retirement planning services.

A one-person wedding consulting business owner may need to have several types of insurance. First, you may need general business liability insurance, which protects you if you are sued for something you did (or didn't do), both in your home office and at wedding/reception sites. However, when you start calling around for insurance, you may discover that many general liability policies are available for low-traffic homebased businesses only. If you plan to conduct bridal consultations in your home frequently, or if you will hire many independent contractors who will actually work at your home, you are likely to need business owner's insurance instead. This type of insurance provides coverage against physical injuries to your customers and employees, damage to the property of others while on your property (such as damage to a bride's car when it's parked in your driveway), and other situations. This kind of coverage is separate from your homeowner's policy and can cost $350 to $450 per year for $500,000 worth of coverage from an independent agent, or $150 to $300 per year for $300,000 worth of coverage from a company like State Farm.

Insurance Riders

If you do choose to work out of a home office, you may wish to increase your homeowners' or apartment insurance coverage to protect your office equipment and furniture. Many companies offer supplemental insurance policies known as riders that are attached to your existing insurance policy. Because they "ride" along with the main policy, your policy doesn't have to be rewritten; you'll just incur an additional charge.

Insurance riders are usually pretty inexpensive. For example, AAA Michigan charges just $30 a year for a $2,000 business equipment replacement rider. The operative word here is "replacement." As you know, used equipment has very little residual value, so a policy that offers replacement coverage is a must.

Commercial Business Insurance

Alternatively, if you decide to establish your wedding consultant business in a location away from your home, you'll need commercial business insurance. The amount of insurance you will need depends on the type of business you run (and generally speaking, liability for a service business like wedding consultation is low), as well as state or municipal regulations. Your insurance agent can guide you in these matters, but you can also contact your local government to find out what the regulations are.

Other Types of Insurance

Last but not least, since you'll be self-employed, you'll also want to consider business interruption insurance, as well as life and health insurance for yourself and your family. The IRS allows self-employed people to deduct the full cost of health

Smart Tip

One last type of insurance you should consider purchasing is professional liability, or errors-and-omissions insurance. It covers you against professional negligence and claims that you didn't perform as promised. It's usually sold in increments of $1 million, with annual premiums of only a few hundred dollars.

insurance for themselves, their spouse, and their dependents as long as a net profit for the year is reported on Schedule C ("Profit or Loss from Business") of their personal tax return. Wedding consultants who form a corporation may also deduct the cost of health insurance, but the reporting situation is different. Consult your accountant if this situation applies to you.

To Insure or Not to Insure

Think you don't need so much insurance? Think again. As one State Farm insurance agent puts it, "The wedding day is a very emotional day—and if the limo is late, the caterer doesn't show up, or something else bad happens, even if it's not the consultant's fault, the wedding couple might choose to sue her anyway."

You may choose to do your own legal and accounting work, but absolutely do not consider operating your business without some type of liability insurance. Even if you are very careful and conscientious, you never know when you will find yourself a party in a lawsuit, or the victim of a break-in, or an act of God like a tornado or earthquake. A low-cost insurance policy could save your business from bankruptcy in the aftermath of any kind of catastrophic loss, either manmade or natural.

Computer Champion

One more business professional you should consider adding to your administrative team is a computer consultant. Because your computer will be the nerve center of your business (keeping your schedule, tracking expenses, and so forth), it deserves its own "doctor" to keep it running in peak condition.

While you can save some money by packing up your computer and lugging it into a computer store every time you need repairs, software updates, or virus checks,

Dollar Stretcher

If you need several different types of business insurance, consider contacting an insurance broker, who can shop around for the best rates. Agents who are aligned with just one company will be locked into its rates, which may be higher than what the competition charges. Check your state's insurance department for a list of reputable brokers.

Professional Services Checklist

Be sure to address these essentials when launching your business:

❑ Consult with an attorney to select the best legal form for your business.

❑ Contact an accountant to discuss the financial and tax requirements related to establishing and operating your business.

❑ Meet with an insurance agent to discuss insurance options and create a custom plan for your business.

❑ Locate a computer consultant who makes house calls and sign up for a service policy, if available.

it's usually a better idea to find a computer expert who makes house calls. Not only will you get on-the-spot service so you'll have less downtime, but you'll also save yourself the frustration of unhooking your computer, then reconnecting it again after it has been serviced.

Computer consultants often offer service contracts that cover an annual tune-up, virus protection, and a set number of service calls. Alternatively, you can hire a tech expert by the hour. Ask your accountant, attorney, and other business colleagues for a lead to a reputable and skilled computer consultant.

Tools and Equipment that Make Dreams Come True

You have the vision and enthusiasm to make wedding days special. You have the dedication and determination to succeed in business. Now all you need are some tools and equipment to get your new wedding consulting business off the ground.

Because most wedding consulting businesses begin as homebased operations, startup costs are relatively low. When you're homebased, you won't have the overhead associated with renting an office space. You probably can use office equipment you already own, like a desktop computer or laptop. Your dining room table will suffice as a desk, at least initially, and your home telephone can pinch hit as your business line until you weigh the options and benefits of landlines, cellphones, or internet phone service (something that should be high on your priority list). You won't even have to invest in an extensive business wardrobe as long as you already own attire that would be appropriate for business meetings, bridal consultations, and on-site wedding coordination.

> **Dollar Stretcher**
> Rummage through your desk drawers before heading out to the office supply store. Hopefully you'll have enough pens, pads, and sticky notes on hand to launch your business. Use the money you save to buy high-quality imprinted stationery and business cards instead.

This chapter will help you take a systematic approach to estimating your startup costs so you'll know whether you need to seek outside financing. But the good news is you should be able to handle the cost using personal savings or plastic. Read on to find out how.

Tools of the Trade

The basics you must have to get your business off the ground include office equipment, furniture and business equipment like computers, and office supplies.

> **Beware!**
> Wedding consultants sometimes rent props like plant stands, chuppahs (the canopy used at Jewish weddings), and aisle runners to create an additional revenue stream. But don't even think about doing that until you've been in business for a while. You don't need the extra financial burden or the hassle of managing props when you're still learning the business.

You'll find a chart on page 63 with estimates of the equipment startup costs for two hypothetical businesses that you can refer to as you estimate your own costs. These businesses include "Weddings by Jamie Lynn," a homebased company with an office set up in the corner of the den. The owner financed the startup with her personal credit cards. The second hypothetical company, "Cherished Moments in Time," has a 500-square-foot office in a commercial building. This business has top-of-the-line equipment and furniture, and employs two contractors to help out with weddings, at a cost of $100 per wedding. "Weddings by

Jamie Lynn" is projecting an annual gross income of $25,000 (10 weddings at $2,500 each), while the owner of "Cherished Moments in Time," expects to earn $62,500 (25 weddings at $2,500 each).

Office Equipment

One of the largest expenditures you'll make at the advent of your new career will be for office furniture. Although you can run your business from a corner of your living room or your dining room table, you'll feel much more productive and professional if you set up a permanent office space in a room or, if space is an issue, a secluded corner of your home. You also must make sure your spouse or significant other and the kids understand that this is a work zone, and that the computer is off limits. Being able to close the door at the end of the work day is a good way to reinforce that message.

If you won't be huddling with brides in your home office, feel free to go "shabby chic" when furnishing your office. Just make sure you have an actual desk at the right height for your computer, a comfortable office chair, and a sturdy two- or four-drawer file cabinet. You should also consider acquiring a bookcase so you can keep your reference materials conveniently at hand.

If you're sadly lacking in the furniture department or you want to make a professional impression on prospective clients, head over to an office supply store like Staples or Office Depot, which sell reasonably priced office furniture that will set you back as little as $176 for a desk and less than $100 and up for a chair. A steel two-drawer letter-size file cabinet starts at about $50, while a wood veneer, four-shelf bookcase costs around $50.

If you're after a more stylish look, head over to your local IKEA or www.ikea.com. The Swedish furniture seller offers attractive pieces at reasonable prices, while OfficeMax offers an extensive line of commercial office furniture that isn't as expensive as you may think. For example, the Mayline Brighton collection, in a natural cherry laminate, includes a stylish desk for $279, a hutch with glass doors for $479, a lateral file cabinet for $400, and a bookcase for $260.

Another viable option for furnishing your office affordably is to scour Craigslist or the local Salvation Army for gently used pieces. Finally, check eBay for deals. A recent auction included a matching double pedestal

Tip...

Smart Tip

A dedicated, uncluttered, toy-free office is a must for consultations held in your home. Brides who will give you thousands of dollars to create their dream wedding definitely won't appreciate meeting at the dining room table. If a home office isn't viable, meet clients in a coffeehouse or restaurant instead—and always pick up the tab.

U-shaped desk and hutch set for $895, with free shipping. But if you buy online, read the fine print so you know exactly what the freight charge will be to get it to you and whether you'll have to assemble it when it arrives.

Personal Computer

A personal computer or laptop is a must for wedding consultants. You'll use it to schedule events, create service proposals, prepare invoices, search the internet for products and vendors to supply them, write letters, and otherwise manage your business. Because computer power is so central to the life of a bridal consultant, you may find that a laptop will serve your purposes better because they're portable. Alternatively, you can buy apps that allow you to open Microsoft Office, pdf, and other files on your smartphone, but of course, a phone is no substitute for a computer that can print files, archive material, and so on. Smartphone productivity apps are discussed in Chapter 12, "Matrimonial Money Matters."

Dell is just one of the many companies that sell affordable and reliable computer systems. For example, at press time, a Dell Inspiron 15R laptop was just $450, while an Inspiron 560 desktop started at $279. Some shoes cost more than that, and they can't even download iTunes or do your taxes. Add on a monitor and a printer and you're looking at only about $700 for a laptop setup, and about $500 for the desktop.

Other useful add-ons include a scanner ($100 and up) and a digital camera ($100 and up). Purchase a camera with 12.0-megapixels or higher, and you'll be able to take photos that will be good enough to post on your website.

> **Smart Tip**
>
> Always buy the best computer chair you can afford. You'll be spending a lot of time in that chair, talking with brides and vendors, coordinating details, and setting schedules. A good office chair will help prevent the dreaded back and sciatica pain that can be triggered by sitting too long in a poorly constructed chair.

> **Dollar Stretcher**
>
> A multifunction printer/scanner/copier like the HP OfficeJet J4580 is a great buy at around $100. Its small footprint makes it compact enough to keep right on your desk within easy reach, and it eliminates the need to buy a bunch of separate peripherals.

Software

Besides Microsoft Office, which you'll use for everyday business tasks, you'll need an accounting software package like Intuit QuickBooks (starting at $229) or Sage Peachtree (starting at $199). Both of these are available online or at office supply and computer stores. Both are discussed in more detail in Chapter 12, "Matrimonial Money Matters."

Wedding professionals also need wedding planning software to organize the myriad details required to deliver big extravaganzas and intimate affairs alike, both on budget and on time. A few software packages to explore include Wedding Management for Professionals (www.weddingmanagement.net, $365), Event Magic Pro (http://frogware.com, $289), iDo Wedding and Event Professional Edition (www.elmsoftware.com, $299), and My Wedding Workbook Professional Edition (www.myweddingworkbook.com, $34 a month to plan up to 20 weddings at a time).

By now it should be obvious that attention to detail is one of the most important personal traits a wedding consultant must have. Make sure you have a calendar and planning app for your smartphone (like Awesome Note + Todo), or a tried-and-true notebook-style planner.

Software for Wedding Consultants

Event Magic Pro (managing the details) and Room Magic Pro (room layout/floorplan) are software programs designed for wedding consultants. According to Kim Roberts of FrogWare, the company that develops this software, Event Magic Pro has complete templates to guide you through the planning process—a big help when you are getting started using the software. The templates can all be customized so you can tailor the software to meet your needs. A really nice unique feature is the Task Reminder list on the Home page. This is a list of all To Do items across all events—a master To Do list. The software also includes invoicing, timelines, checklists (for client and consultant), budgets, pie charts, vendor comparisons, table assignments, wedding day agendas, wedding party reports, menu selections, and more. You can also email all of the information/reports.

Room Magic Pro allows you to do the layout for the events (reception, rehearsal dinner, etc). The system does the initial layout for you based on the room dimensions, number of people attending, types of tables, and spacing requirements.

Event Magic Pro was designed by consultants; FrogWare was approached by consultants and asked to develop the program. The first version was released in 1997. There are at least two releases of the software per year, all of which are driven by customer requests.

Event Magic Pro is $289, and Room Magic Pro is $69. There is a free demo on the website—simply download and try the full program free for 30 days.

Keep Track of Expenses

Just about anything you purchase for use in your business is deductible on your federal income taxes, provided you have the proper written documentation (like receipts and packing slips). The Section 179 expense deduction will currently allow you to deduct up to $20,000 a year for equipment costs, including computers, office furniture, telecommunications equipment (phones, answering machines, telephone headsets), and fax machines. Other incidentals needed to run your business, like office supplies and professional journals and trade magazines, are also deductible. If any of these items are used for both business and pleasure (like your kids using the PC to research dinosaurs for a school project), you can only deduct the amount of time the computer is actually in service for the business. The IRS recommends keeping a log showing business vs. personal usage.

Happily, other costs typically incurred by wedding consultants, including professional fees for attorneys and CPAs, advertising and marketing costs, business equipment repairs, voice mail, seminars required to improve business skills, trade show and conference fees, and bank fees, may be written off against your business taxes.

Check with your accountant for details and to make sure you are following all current tax laws. The IRS keeps a close eye on at-home businesses, particularly tracking if home offices are being used for business as well as pleasure. Don't fudge these numbers. It is in your best interest to have accurate numbers and a careful log of office space and use if the IRS comes calling.

Beware!

No matter how tempting, never put a client on hold to answer another incoming call—this is what your answering machine is for. The client you put on hold will likely be offended if you shunt her off for another phone call.

Fax Machines

Fax machines may be considered old technology, but they're still handy to have, especially if you'll be faxing orders and confirmations to vendors, and it's still a good idea to keep one on its own dedicated telephone line. That way, your computer (which likely came with a fax card) doesn't have to be running for you to send or receive a fax 24/7. You can get a plain paper fax machine for as little as $60 or a multifunction (fax/scanner/printer) for about $100.

Telephones and Answering Machines

Be sure to invest a few Benjamins on a good-quality business phone because you'll be using it constantly. For example, a two-line, Polycom SoundPoint IP speakerphone, which has a great sound clarity and is VoIP-compatible, runs $239. In addition to office supply stores, you can find a wide range of professional business phones at Hello Direct (www.hellodirect.com).

Voice mail is great, but sometimes you just want to screen those incoming calls so you don't have to talk to too many telemarketers or all of your kids' friends. Answering machines cost as little as $20, or to keep your desk uncluttered, pick a business phone with a built-in answering machine (about $150).

Cellular Phone

A cell phone is a must for wedding consultants. Period. If you don't have one or yours is out of date, put it at the top of your business equipment wish list.

BlackBerry and iPhone

You don't need all the bells and whistles you'll get with an iPhone or Android phone, but they do have apps that make life easier. An iPhone 4G lists for $449, but you can get a 3G phone for much less and a basic BlackBerry for way less than that—even free, with certain data plans. A flip phone, which doesn't have the "ill" factor (teenspeak for "cool") of an iPhone, but does have updated features, retails for less than $50.

Copy Machines

No one says you need a copy machine right in your office, especially when quickie print shops like FedEx Office, Staples, or American Speedy Printing are so conveniently located all around the country. But you can't beat the convenience of having your own copier right at your side, especially since they cost as little as $400 for a desktop model.

Dollar Stretcher
You may be able to deduct a percentage of your mortgage payment, utility bills, etc., as a home business expense. Use Form 8829, "Expenses for the Business Use of Your Home," to determine the allowable amount, then report it on Schedule C. Or better yet, ask your accountant to do the deed for you.

Toner cartridges run about $80 and deliver thousands of copies.

Internet Postage and Postage Meters

Eliminate trips to the post office by purchasing postage online. If you expect to be a frequent mailer (it could happen if you choose to solicit new business using direct mail), you may want to consider leasing a postage meter at a cost of about $20 per month, plus the cost of postage and supplies. One to investigate: mailstation2 from PitneyBowes (www.pb.com), which comes with a 60-day trial and free postage when you sign up.

You certainly can use a postage machine to affix postage to wedding invitations, but of course, that doesn't have the same je ne sais quoi as a stamp. So either order stamps online that bear the photo of your bride and her intended, or order "Love" and wedding stamps (with photos of a wedding cake or a pair of wedding rings) directly from the U.S. Postal Service at www.usps.com. In any event, you probably should lay in a supply of the wedding stamps for your own use since they're representative of what you'll be doing for a living.

Finally, you can print Priority or Express Mail postage right on your desktop using Click-N-Ship through the U.S. Postal Service. All you need is the USPS Shipping Assistant (free at www.usps.com) and Click-n-Ship labels (from $7 for 50 Priority Mail labels).

You'll need a postal scale to make sure you're affixing enough postage to your outgoing mail. A 5-pound digital postage scale for both letters and packages runs under $35, while a 10-pound scale is less than $70 at office supply stores.

> **Bright Idea**
> Play soft, tasteful music in the background when you record your answering machine or voice mail message. Some classical selections that will give your message wedding ambience include "Canon in D" by Pachelbel, or "Air on the G String" by Johann Sebastian Bach.

> **Bright Idea**
> Give wedding invitations a customized look by using personalized postage that features the happy couple's picture on the stamps. A sheet of 20 first-class stamps starts at about $18 and is available from U.S. Postal Service-approved vendors like PitneyBowes and www.zazzle.com, among others.

Office Supplies

In addition to the ordinary items you'll need to run your business, from yellow legal pads to copy paper, you'll need good-quality imprinted stationery and business cards. Print shops like FedEx Office, office supply stores like Office Depot and Staples, and online printers like Vistaprint (www.

vistaprint.com) can whip up professional-looking custom stationery for you at a reasonable cost (starting at about $100 for 250 raised letter sheets, $40 for 500 envelopes, and $20 for 250 business cards). As a general rule, you should stick with stationery in white, cream, or gray for an elegant, conservative look.

This stationery runs under $6 for a package of 100 sheets of stationery, under $8 for 50 envelopes, and under $7 for 250 business cards. As far as other office supply costs go, you should figure on spending about $150, which will buy pens, pads, copy paper, file folders, and the like.

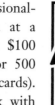

Beware!

Have your business stationery and cards professionally printed. Avoid purchasing blank stationery and business cards from an office supply store and printing your own on your office printer.

The Final Tally

If you've been noting your estimated costs on the "Office Equipment and Supplies" worksheet on page 64 as you read this chapter, you should now have a pretty good idea of how much capital you might need to cover those costs. If you need some guidance or inspiration, take a look at the "Startup Expenses" chart on page 65 for a tally of what the overall startup costs would be to get two hypothetical wedding consultant businesses off the ground.

Armed with that information, use the "Startup Expenses" worksheet on page 66 to get a clearer picture of what your total expenses might be. Some of the costs on the worksheet can be estimated from the figures discussed in previous chapters, including the costs associated with market research (refer to Chapter 3), licenses (Chapter 4), and attorney, accountant, and insurance costs (Chapter 5). In Chapter 8, you'll get an idea about what it costs for certification, training, subscriptions, and dues for professional organizations. Advertising costs will be addressed in Chapter 9, and online service and website design and hosting costs will be covered in Chapter 10.

Bright Idea

Raised letter printing (known as thermography) or gold foil stamping may cost a little more, but they add an elegant touch to your stationery and business cards. For the very best look, have your stationery printed on laid bond paper. It has the smoothest surface of all printing papers and produces the crispest printed images.

In addition to the costs listed here, you'll have other ongoing monthly expenses once your business is up and running. See Chapter 12 for a discussion of these costs, as well as some advice on approaching bankers and obtaining financing.

Office Equipment and Supplies

Below are the office equipment and supplies costs for two hypothetical wedding consulting businesses. The cost of essential equipment for "Cherished Moments in Time," such as the computer/printer and office furniture, is doubled because this hypothetical business employs a contract administrative helper.

	Weddings by Jamie Lynn	Cherished Moments in Time
Office equipment		
Computer, printer	—	$1,400
Software		
Microsoft Office	$280	$560
Intuit QuickBooks	—	$229
Wedding software	$289	$365
Multipurpose fax/scanner/copier	—	$100
Digital camera	$100	$150
Fax machine	—	—
Copy machine	—	$400
Phone	$75	$300
Cell phone	$50	$100
Answering machine	$20	—
Postage meter	—	—
Digital postage scale	—	—
Office furniture		
Desk	$200	$800
Chair	$100	$400
File cabinet(s)	$50	$400
Bookcase(s)	—	—
Office supplies		
Letterhead, envelopes, business cards	$160	$160
Brochures	$325	$325
Miscellaneous supplies (pens, folders, etc.)	$30	$50
Computer/copier paper	$35	$35
Extra printer cartridges (black)	$35	$70
Extra copier toner cartridge	—	$80
CD-RW disks	$15	$15
Total	**$1,764**	**$5,939**

Office Equipment and Supplies Worksheet

Item	Cost
Office equipment	
Computer, printer	$
Software	
Microsoft Office	$
Intuit QuickBooks	$
Wedding software	$
Multipurpose fax/scanner/copier	$
Digital camera	$
Fax machine	$
Copy machine	$
Phone	$
Cell phone	$
Answering machine	$
Postage meter	$
Digital postage scale	$
Office furniture	
Desk	$
Chair	$
File cabinet(s)	$
Bookcase(s)	$
Office supplies	
Letterhead, envelopes, business cards	$
Brochures	$
Miscellaneous supplies (pens, folders, etc.)	$
Computer/copier paper	$
Extra printer cartridges (black)	$
Extra copier toner cartridge	$
CD-RW disks	$
Total	$

Startup Expenses

Here are the startup expenses for our two hypothetical wedding consultant businesses:

	Weddings by Jamie Lynn (low)	Cherished Moments in Time (high)
Startup Expenses		
Mortgage/rent (first six months)	$0	$3,000
Utilities (one month deposit)		
Maintenance (first six months)		$600
Phone (line installation charge)	$40	$80
Office equipment, furniture, supplies	$1,764	$6,199
Business licenses	$20	$20
Business insurance (annual cost)	$1,200	$1,200
Employee/contractor wages (first six months)		$3,990
Benefits/taxes		
Startup advertising	$250	$500
Legal services	$120	$900
Accounting services (first six months)		$900
Membership dues	$175	$240
Publications (annual subscriptions)	$17	$200
Online services (Broadband)	$40	$40
Website design	$1,000	$2,500
Web hosting, domain name (annual cost)	$72	$72
Subtotal	$4,698	$20,441
Miscellaneous expenses (roughly 10 percent of total)	$470	$2,050
Total	**$5,168**	**$22,491**

Startup Expenses Worksheet

Item	Cost
Startup Expenses	
Mortgage/rent (first six months)	$
Utilities (one month deposit)	$
Maintenance (first six months)	$
Phone (line installation charge)	$
Office equipment, furniture, supplies	$
Business licenses	$
Business insurance (annual cost)	$
Employee/contractor wages (first six months)	$
Benefits/taxes	$
Startup advertising	$
Legal services	$
Accounting services (first six months)	$
Membership dues	$
Publications (annual subscriptions)	$
Online services (Broadband)	$
Website design	$
Web hosting, domain name (annual cost)	$
Subtotal	$
Miscellaneous expenses (roughly 10 percent of total)	$
Total	**$**

7

Establishing a Vendor Network

One of the things that will make you valuable to your customer is your knowledge of the bridal industry. As a consultant, you are expected to be the font from which all knowledge about the industry flows. That means knowing things like which wedding gown styles or decorating schemes are in vogue

▲

and which are passé, or whether it's inspired or gauche to use silk flowers in the bride's bouquet.

But perhaps even more important, your clients will count on you to recommend reliable vendors that offer the best quality and value for their money. So it's your job to research bridal service providers in your target market area to find the best possible sources for the products or services you'll require. From this research, you should compile a list of preferred vendors you can either share with the bride during a consultation or use yourself if you're in charge of all the planning.

Smart Tip

When researching reception sites, don't limit your prospect list to traditional wedding banquet facilities. Hotels, country clubs, resorts, and historic sites (like Mary Gay House, an 1820 antebellum home in Decatur, Georgia) make lovely sites for weddings and provide a wider range of price choices for the bride.

Although this process can be rather time consuming, it's essential for your future success. Every time you recommend a vendor, you're putting your own reputation on the line, so you'll want to make sure your suppliers have impeccable credentials and excellent reputations.

Finding Reputable Suppliers

The easiest way to identify potential service providers is by asking around for recommendations. "Get referrals from recently married friends, family, business associates, and clients," says Deborah McCoy, president of the American Academy of Wedding Professionals. "When aspiring consultants start asking for referrals, they'll find that the same names—both good and bad—pop up over and over. It's then up to the consultant to build relationships with quality vendors."

Other useful sources of information include the internet and the local chamber of commerce. The Better Business Bureau can also be useful for helping you steer clear of businesses whose reputations are less than sterling. Check the Bureau's online directory of accredited businesses at www.bbb.org for the 411 on local vendors.

In this initial fact-finding stage, don't limit yourself to locating a certain number of vendors. Rather, identify as many potential sources as possible so you'll have several to choose from when the time comes to make a recommendation to a bride. Keep in mind, too, that you should locate vendors in the low, medium, and high price ranges to accommodate all budgets.

Then once you have compiled your list of sources, pick up the phone and make appointments to see vendors' facilities and products in person. Since business owners are generally pleased to grant you a personal interview and show off their services and/ or products as a way to secure future business, those who balk should be removed from your list.

Go to each interview armed with a list of specific questions concerning the company's scope of services, prices, delivery schedules, terms, and so on. Don't rely on your memory to keep the details straight; eventually there will come a point when you've talked to or seen so many vendors you won't remember who's who. Instead, create a simple form on your computer that you can fill out as you interview potential sources, or use the iPhone notes app to jot down pertinent information. Besides full contact information, be sure to note the business's hours of operation and location.

In addition, Robbi Ernst III of June Wedding Inc. says, "Business licenses, appropriate insurance, contracts, health permits for food providers, years in business, number of weddings worked on, and the ability to work well with other professionals should be at the top of your list when gathering information about vendors."

Once your inspections are completed, evaluate providers in each category against one another and rank them based on quality, value, timely delivery, and so on. Finally, check their business references to verify their reputations and reliability. The top-ranked vendors become your preferred suppliers, although you can always add to this list as you hear about other promising vendors. Identifying numerous vendors in each category has another advantage: You'll always have someone prescreened and ready to go if your top choice is already booked.

As you get your business established, you should expect your supplier list to change. You'll always add new vendors as well as remove those that don't live up to your expectations.

"I constantly shop for vendors, so I have a large resource library that I can refer to based on the bride's preferences, personality, budget, and vendor availability," says Paula Laskelle, a wedding consultant in San Clemente, California.

Major Suppliers

Wedding consultants need a whole phalanx of reliable suppliers to help create the wedding of brides' dreams. Among them are reception facility managers, caterers, florists, DJs, photographers, limousine companies, and others. Here's a look at each of these crucial dream-makers.

The Host with the Most

Receptions these days can be held anywhere, from a traditional banquet facility to a beachfront pavilion, a historic inn, or a theme park like Walt Disney World. The key to a spectacular event is a good working relationship with the reception site manager, since he or she can make the difference between a good and a spectacular function.

When vetting reception site managers, be sure to inquire about the number of people the venue can accommodate, the cost per guest, the number of hours the facility can be rented for, and the type of food it provides. Ask, too, about any restrictions there may be on the wedding party and their guests (such as a lack of handicapped facilities, or a ban on smoking or alcohol, a situation you will encounter at some outdoor park sites).

Keep in mind that many banquet facilities offer full-service packages that include food, a wedding cake, a photographer, and a videographer, so you might be required to select from the facility's own preferred vendor list. If that's the case and you prefer to use your own sources, you should take your reception business elsewhere.

Finally, ask for permission to visit the facility during a wedding to observe the wait staff and the management in action, as well as the general operation of the business. You should also ask to sample any food provided for a typical wedding dinner. In many cases, the bridal couple may wish to be part of the fun, so be sure to clear that with the site manager rather than just showing up with them in tow.

These days, nontraditional sites are becoming more common for both the nuptials and receptions. According to Gerard J. Monaghan of the Association of Bridal Consultants, alternative locations like gardens are quite popular, as are luxury hotels where the ceremony and reception can be held in the same place (think Las Vegas). The trend to hold weddings in unusual locales also continues, while receptions at private estates are especially popular in California, according to Ann Nola of the Association of Certified Professional Wedding Consultants.

"There are now so many scuba weddings that several companies manufacture white wet suits," Monaghan adds. "You name it, someone is doing it."

Contact your local chamber of commerce or county seat for a list of places (like restaurants and parks) that allow weddings at their facilities. Remember that a permit may be required, and there may be other restrictions, such as a ban on alcoholic beverages or extremely loud music.

Fanciful Feasts

Although many reception halls and other sites have their own caterers, it's still a good idea to establish your own network of caterers, especially for weddings in nontraditional settings. As with banquet facilities, you will want to talk to prospective catering sources about menus, specialties, and price ranges. You'll also want to find out if they can fulfill special requests (such as preparing kosher or vegetarian cuisine), and whether they provide linen, china, and glassware. Then ask permission to drop in on a function they're catering to sample the cuisine and observe the service.

Exciting Food Trends

From comfort food favorites to more adventurous fare, wedding food has moved way beyond traditional plated meals to become as trendy and hip as wedding couples themselves. Here's a look at some of the hottest food finds for the millennial+10 generation:

○ *Martini mashed potato bars.* Guests create their own potato "cocktail" side dishes in martini glasses. Haute cuisine toppings include imported cheeses, crab and shrimp sauce, and even caviar. A hot variation on this theme is the mac-and-cheese "martinis," which are made with gourmet cheeses and garnished with lobster, andouille sauce, and other delectable toppings.

○ *Tapas, canapés, and other small bites.* Especially those cradled in edible vessels like fluted tortilla cones or mini bread bowls. They're easier to eat and allow guests to mingle more efficiently.

○ *Sushi stations.* Although not for every taste, raw bars are colorful, hip—and pricey. And because not everyone loves sushi, be sure to offer other types of nibbles so everyone is happy.

○ *Food trucks and vending carts.* Although not the main menu attraction, gourmet food trucks and carts are pulling up during cocktail hour or at after-parties to serve waffles, tacos, and even fully-loaded Coney Island hot dogs. It's a great way to take the edge off any alcohol-fueled partying.

○ *Main-dish cupcakes.* Savory meat "cupcakes" frosted with delicately flavored mashed potatoes and other toppings have invaded cocktail hour. But never fear, cupcake wedding cakes are still in vogue, although they've received a gourmet makeover. One of the trendy new favorites: individual chocolate tortes with an artful sprinkling of sea salt.

Floral Fantasies

Flowers are an integral part of a wedding, so it's essential to select florists who can deliver floral designs that are both beautiful and imaginative. Toomie Farris, president of McNamara Florist in Indianapolis, Indiana, and an FTD Master Designer, says the best florists are the ones who take the time to understand the bride's vision for her special day, then translate that feeling into a coordinated floral display.

"I never let a bride or her wedding consultant jump immediately into details like picking which bouquet she wants," Farris says. "It's more important to understand the entire event and the overall feel of the wedding, based on the bride's personal taste and the way she expresses herself."

Toward that end, when you interview florists, ask them about their approach to designing a coordinated wedding package. Although flowers make up a large chunk of the bridal budget (averaging $1,970, according to the Bridal Association of America), a good florist can work wonders even on a small budget. For example, Farris says a simple table arrangement consisting of a large Monstera leaf sprayed with metallic paint and accented with bear grass and a few sprigs of fern has a high-style look, yet costs under $25 to create.

Florists can usually show you portfolios of their work to give you an idea of what they can do, but it's also a good idea to take a peek in the cooler to check the freshness of the floral product. Note particularly whether the water in the buckets is crystal clear, which indicates the flowers have been processed properly for maximum freshness.

Also, florists who specialize in wedding flowers usually can provide special table linens, runners, arches, pedestals, candles and tableware, place cards, chair covers and bows, cake "jewelry" and cake stands, and wedding favors.

And just as a side note: Balloons are definitely out. Farris says they're tacky and belong at baby showers, not elegant weddings.

The Sound of Music

Unless you are a real audiophile who keeps up with the latest iPod tunes and musical trends, you should seek the help of a professional entertainment consultant to find bands that provide reception music. These consultants will have audition tapes on file to make the job of selecting musicians easier, but it's usually wiser to see the band perform live so you're not unpleasantly surprised by either the quality of their work or their physical appearance on the big day. Other sources for recommendations

The Language of Flowers

Here are the secret messages of love attached to some commonly used wedding flowers:

- ○ Alstoremeria: devotion
- ○ Baby's breath: pure of heart
- ○ Calla lily: beauty
- ○ Camellia: excellence, beauty
- ○ Carnation, white: perfect loveliness
- ○ Chrysanthemum, white: truth
- ○ Daisy: innocence
- ○ Delphinium: open heart and deep attachment
- ○ Gardenia: refinement
- ○ Lily of the Valley: return of happiness
- ○ Magnolia: magnificence
- ○ Lily, white: sweetness and purity
- ○ Orchid: love and beauty
- ○ Ranunculus: radiant with charm
- ○ Rose, red: I love you
- ○ Rose, white: purity and love
- ○ Rosebud, red: pure and lovely
- ○ Stephanotis: happiness in marriage
- ○ Tulip, red: love
- ○ Violet: faithfulness

Sources: FTD, USA Bride

are banquet managers, and anyone whose opinion you respect who works on site with bands, such as photographers and caterers.

Ideally, your supplier "play list" should consist of several bands that can pull off everything from big band music to young country. But it's more realistic to expect

Smart Tip

Tip...

Always strongly discourage couples who are trying to save money by having "iPod" reception music. A reception needs a master of ceremonies to direct the after-dinner activities. Also, according to the American Disc Jockey Association, the cost of an iPod, PA system, and iTunes wedding music pack is just slightly less than the services of a professional disc jockey.

your musicians to specialize in certain types of music. Generally speaking, a band that can play both rock and easy listening music will be suitable for most audiences.

Another viable option that is easier on the budget but is a potentially more versatile musical choice is a disc jockey. You can easily find DJs listed in the Yellow Pages under "Bands," "Music," or "Weddings," or ask friends and acquaintances for recommendations. There are also sites on the internet that can steer you toward a DJ. Two reputable sites to try are 1-800-DISC JOCKEY at www.800dj.com and the American Disc Jockey Association at www.adja.org.

A good DJ will come prepared to handle special requests in many categories. Ask potential vendors for a list of the music he or she typically brings to a reception.

Say Cheese

Good photography is truly an art, so you'll want to screen prospective photographers very carefully. To locate photographers, try the Yellow Pages or an online search. The Professional Photographers of America Inc. (www.ppa.com) can provide you with potential sources, but keep in mind that these are just leads, not recommendations. Talk to banquet facility managers for referrals to experienced shutterbugs.

When reviewing a photographer's portfolio, note the settings and lighting conditions under which the snapshots were taken. Some photographers are more adept at interior photography than garden settings, for instance, just as some are more skilled at taking candids vs. portraits. Each type of photographer has his or her place on your supplier list.

You'll also want to assess the photographer's people skills, since he or she will be interacting constantly with the bride and groom. Look for someone who is professional, yet warm and friendly, and be

Fun Fact

In the South, it's customary to display wedding photos of the happy couple at the reception. Since these photos are taken before the big day in full wedding regalia, there must not be anything to the old wives' tale that it's bad luck for the groom to see the bride before the wedding!

sure to ask what he or she wears while working. Formal weddings require formal attire for vendors like the photographer, too.

Lights, Camera, Action!

As with photographers, you must view a videographer's work before adding him or her to your list of preferred suppliers. It's important to ascertain whether the sample footage you see was actually shot by that person or by an assistant. It's a good idea to ask for recommendations from people who regularly use videographers, such as banquet facility managers, and even other vendors. You want a professional who will be discreet and won't interfere with either the ceremony or reception. Above all, this means no bright lights and no pushy behavior to get just the right angle.

Finally, determine whether the videographer shoots just raw footage, or whether he or she will edit it and add an appropriate musical score. Obviously, the latter is more time-consuming and expensive and requires more expertise.

Sweet Endings

Locating a good baker certainly will be one of the tastier aspects of your vendor search. You can ask reputable caterers and other wedding suppliers for leads, or consult the "Confectionary Artist" listing at the International Cake Exploration Societé's website (www.ices.org). Additional sources of wedding confectionary include the pastry chefs at upscale restaurants and banquet facilities, which may even do the baking and decorating on-site.

In addition to poring over prospective vendors' portfolios of cake designs, visit The Knot's wedding cake gallery of more than 1,000 elegant, imaginative and creative cakes at www.theknot.com for inspiration. Once you've narrowed down your vendor list, always ask to sample the offerings. Inquire, too, about the availability of cake accessories like toppers, pedestals, traditional fountains, and chocolate fountains, all of which give the cake a custom look.

In some parts of the country (notably the South), a groom's cake is a charming tradition. The groom's cake is generally richer and denser than the bride's cake, and is often sliced and wrapped in ribbon-

Beware!

Some religious denominations do not allow videographers to film during the wedding ceremony—or they may be required to work at a discreet distance. So always check with the pastor or another church official to make sure filming is permissible, as well as to find out whether the videographer may set up lights or other equipment in the sanctuary.

Smart Tip

Tip...

One way to get viable leads on vendors is to ask each supplier you interview who he or she likes to work with. When you start to hear the same names over and over, you can assume those vendors are reliable and will provide consistent service.

tied boxes so guests can carry pieces home to enjoy later. Another charming southern tradition calls for the baker to hide charms attached to ribbons in the cake. Before the cake is cut, each bridesmaid pulls a ribbon to remove a small token like a four-leaf clover, which is a symbol of good luck, or a ring, which signifies the next to marry. Keep in mind, however, that some state laws prohibit the baking of inedible objects in cakes, so be sure to check state regulations before you offer such a service to a bride.

Cinderella's Coach

A bride's special day calls for the special transportation provided by a limousine service. Limousines are usually rented by the hour (with a three-hour minimum) and often provide amenities like champagne. It goes without saying that it's important to locate a reputable limousine company because the safety of your clients and their families is at stake. And beware: Packy Boukis, the wedding consultant in Cleveland, Ohio, warns that limousine companies are notorious for not holding up their end of the contract.

"A family member once used a limousine company that brought in an out-of-town driver to help with the summer crush of weddings," Boukis says. "The driver didn't have a clue where he was going, plus it was 90 degrees that day, and the air conditioning in the limousine was broken. Obviously, this couple didn't ask for any referrals from their sister-in-law, who was their wedding consultant!"

To avoid this kind of problem, contact the National Limousine Association at (800) 652-7007 or www.nlaride.com for a list of preferred service providers. Once you've narrowed down the list in your area, call the limo service's references—all of them—and check the Better Business Bureau's location guide at www.bbb.org to make sure there aren't any negative strikes against the company. Finally, always inspect the company's vehicles to assess their general condition, upkeep, and size, then be sure to get a copy of the signed service contract to avoid any unpleasant surprises later.

Bright Idea

Horse-drawn carriages and vintage trolleys make charming conveyances for the bridal party. An added benefit: They can be used as a backdrop or "prop" for wedding photographs. As a special gift to the bride and groom, stock them with gourmet chocolates, champagne, and special hors d'oeuvres so they don't arrive at the reception hungry.

8

Certification and Professional Development

Search the course catalog for any major university in the United States and you'll see degree programs that teach people a wide variety of skills, including how to package and move objects, how to perform open-heart surgery, and how to run corporations. What you won't find there is a curriculum that specifically teaches a person how to become a wedding consultant.

Smart Tip

Tip...

Having a mentor who can advise you during your startup phases is a great way to help ensure your success. The SBA recommends selecting someone who is experienced, successful, and willing to help you without personal gain. Try the SBA and SCORE (see Appendix) for general assistance, and one of the wedding consultant associations for industry-specific help.

Yet wedding consultants need many of the same business skills that other professionals routinely acquire at universities and colleges. These are skills they use every day for project management, personnel administration, financial planning, even logistics. That's why, over the years, the denizens of the wedding consultant industry have created their own professional certification and training programs. No doubt this was done in part to combat the misconception that wedding consultants were merely bored housewives or terminally perky people who planned their own weddings and loved the experience so much they just had to start businesses of their own.

"Those people are 'dabblers' who simply appropriate the title of 'professional,'" says Robbi Ernst III, president and founder of June Wedding Inc. "Many of today's consultants have experience in wedding-related businesses such as catering or event planning, and it's that kind of experience that makes them successful wedding consultants."

While a college business degree is definitely a plus for anyone planning to start a small business, it's not an absolute necessity. After all, it's not uncommon for business owners of all kinds to hire professionals like accountants or public relations officers to handle tasks they don't have experience with. You can do the same thing. Then in addition to relying on your own common sense and innate intelligence, you should consider taking professional development courses and earning certifications to fill in any gaps in your knowledge.

"The wedding consultant is the expert, and if you are going to be an expert in this industry, you have to know as much as possible on all levels," says Packy Boukis, the Ohio wedding consultant. "I suggest you take as many courses as you can afford."

Deborah McCoy, president of the American Academy of Wedding Professionals, a certification program, agrees. "It is critical that anyone embarking on this

Dollar Stretcher

Many of the wedding consulting associations offer a wide range of membership benefits, including the use of the organization's logo in literature and advertising, merchant credit card acceptance programs, discounts on bridal show booth space, group rates on insurance, and even discounts on rental cars.

career become educated and certified," she says emphatically.

In addition, brides and grooms themselves are helping to push the need for education and certification. Thanks to the internet, savvy couples are able to investigate the wedding professionals they hire very thoroughly, right down to reading testimonials from both satisfied and dissatisfied clients. Having those coveted certification initials after your name will help to give them confidence that you are professional and capable.

Here's a look at some of the associations, certifications, professional development programs, and publications available today to help you excel in you new chosen profession.

> ## Smart Tip
> **Tip...**
>
> When you're deciding on a wedding consultant course, check the credentials of the instructor, says Deborah McCoy, president of the American Academy of Wedding Professionals, a certification program. You want to learn from a bona fide wedding consultant who plans weddings for a living and knows the ins and outs of the business.

Major Industry Associations

There are a number of well-established wedding consultant associations that deserve a look. They include the following.

Association of Bridal Consultants (ABC)

Founded in 1955, ABC is an international association with 4,000 members worldwide. It offers members professional designations at the novice, consultant, and professional levels, as well as accredited designations. Training begins with a five-part home-study course with coursework in etiquette, sales and marketing, the wedding day, related services, and planning and consulting. The cost of the five-part program is $475; it's also possible to take each course individually at a cost of $119 each. Membership dues start at $185 (plus a one-time $35 processing fee) for a novice wedding planner membership.

ABC also offers its Business of Brides Annual Conference, a major international meeting, each November, as well as one- and two-day educational seminars at locations around the United States and Canada. Seminars include "New Horizons" for individuals interested in a career in the wedding industry and the "Expanding Horizons" series for beginners and those who wish to increase their skills. Members also receive a bimonthly newsletter, *ABC Dialogue*, and enjoy other benefits like a

▲

brochure-design critique service, job placement assistance, and more. Visit www. bridalassn.com for more information.

Association of Certified Professional Wedding Consultants (ACPWC)

Based in San Jose, California, ACPWC was founded in 1990 by Ann Nola. It offers a personalized four- or five-day self-directed home-study course. The personalized course is presented by experienced professionals and is held at various locations around the country. It covers everything from the business of wedding consulting to finances, client relations, wedding protocol, and more. The fee is $1,295 both the five-day program and the home-study program. You become eligible for membership in the organization after successful completion of one of the programs.

After earning a certificate of completion, ACPWC members may progress to professional, then certified status. The certified status is awarded only after members achieve professional status, coordinate 12 or more weddings, and obtain eight letters of recommendation. For more information, go to http://acpwc.com.

June Wedding Inc. (JWI)

Founded by Robbi Ernst III, JWI, an Association for Event Professionals is a Guerneville, California-based organization that awards the "JWIC" professional certification to those who complete either a self-certification home-study or on-site training and education course. The "Wedding Consultant: Beginner Course" covers everything you need to set up, design, and run a successful business, including the fundamentals of owning your own business, budgeting, marketing, geographic research, and more. The cost of the beginner course is $1,000. The annual membership dues are $175 for a small business/sole proprietorship, or $275 for corporate membership. More information is available at http://jwidallas.org.

Other Educational Opportunities

While you can't earn a traditional academic degree in wedding consulting, there are a couple of academic institutions that offer the closest thing to a sheepskin. The first is Ashworth College, which has an online course that leads to a career diploma in bridal consulting. Go to www.ashworthcollege.edu for more information. The second, Penn Foster Career School of Scranton, Pennsylvania, offers a wedding planner accreditation program that is completed entirely online. Graduates of the Penn Foster program complete the Association of Bridal Consultants professional certification examination and qualify for a free three-month trial membership in the organization. Tuition is $698 and a payment plan is available. See www.pennfoster.edu for more details.

Industry Certification

Other organizations that offer wedding consulting certification include:

Smart Tip

Tip...

Community colleges often allow entrepreneurs to take a few classes without enrolling in a degree program, and tuition is usually quite reasonable. You may even be able to audit a class for no grade (although this also means your class work won't be evaluated). Entry-level coursework in areas like management, accounting, communication, and marketing are useful for startup business owners.

- *Weddings Beautiful.* This membership association (www.weddingsbeautiful.com) has been providing certification for wedding planners since 1968. It offers two certification levels: certified wedding specialist and certified wedding planner. The certified wedding specialist coursework is completed online at a cost of $695. After coordinating a minimum of 10 weddings and obtaining six references, members can take a test and progress to the certified wedding planner level. Membership in this organization is a bargain at $16 and provides numerous member benefits.

- *Wedding Consultant Certification Institute (WCCI).* Offering a training school and follow-up for new or aspiring wedding planners, WCCI is perfect for individuals who haven't yet launched their business. It offers four education choices: home-study courses, in-person classes, live online classes, and personalized online "WT41" classes, which stands for "Wedding Training for One." The latter are offered to students who are unable to participate in the real-time classes. The home-study course is $695, while the in-person classes cost $595, and the online classes are $349. See www.weddingconsultantcertificationinstitute.com for more information.

No matter which route you take toward educational enlightenment, industry experts like Robbi Ernst stress that investing in your own education is the surest way to becoming a successful wedding consultant. "We have done surveys that show that wedding consultants who are formally trained and certified can get higher fees from the onset of their business if they are professional and know what they're doing," Ernst says. "My strongest advice to anyone starting in this business is to seek out the best and most competent professional training in the industry.

▲

Certification: One Path to Success

Robbi Ernst, president of June Wedding Inc. (JWI), knows the value of wedding consultant education and certification, having been a wedding consultant himself for three decades.

"The information that's imparted in these courses is information that really works in real-life situations," Ernst says. "An advantage of JWI's course is that it's not just a correspondence course. There are three telephone consultations in the program so the student has genuine human interaction with an instructor and can ask questions or ask for clarification right away rather than having to wait for an email or a written critique sent through the mail. They can also get ongoing follow-up technical support and help at no charge as long as they remain a member in good standing."

Ernst points out that the wedding industry has changed significantly over the years, so the need for professional development has changed, too. "When I started out in this industry, wedding consultants were not much more than people who sold invitations, did calligraphy, wrapped almonds in tulle, and such," he says. "I founded JWI because I had a different vision. I saw the need for a true professional and intelligent consultant who knew how to give good guidance to a bride. What the JWI home-study course has done for the industry is to create consistency. You can call a JWI-trained and certified consultant in Boise, Chicago, New York, or Dallas and get a similar professional response from each of them."

The experts can teach you how not to make the mistakes they made, which can save you a small fortune."

Industry Publications

Another way to get educated and stay current on news, information, events, and trends in the wedding industry is by subscribing to publications that serve both the consultant and the consumer. Here's a brief rundown on some of the best-known publications that can keep you plugged into this dynamic industry.

Trade Publications

- *Vows magazine*. This publication, which comes out six times a year, is available only to the bridal trade and provides information that runs the gamut from industry trends to customer service and business techniques. The subscription cost is $25 per year. See http://vowsmagazine.com.
- *WedLock*. This online publication includes access to interactive forums and monthly webinars as part of its subscription cost. An annual subscription is $350, but you can try it out for as little as $69 for two-month access to its resources at www.wedlockmag.com.

Consumer Publications

- *Brides magazine*. This is the premier wedding guide for brides that's instantly recognizable, thanks to its doorstop-sized issues, some of which have more than 1,000 pages. This magazine is published six times a year. The subscription price is $16.95, or two years for $28. It's a must read for keeping up on wedding trends and products. Visit www.brides.com. *Brides* also publishes quarterly special issues known as *Brides Local Magazines* for 16 metro areas and states, including Atlanta, Boston, Colorado, Connecticut, Michigan, northern and southern California, and Washington, DC. The issues are available for $4.95 on newsstands and online at www.brides.com/brides-local.
- *Destination Weddings & Honeymoons*. Published five times a year, this magazine calls itself the "ultimate travel magazine for brides and grooms." It covers everything, from exotic and luxurious destinations to general information about wedding style and accoutrements. The $19.97 subscription also includes an annual worldwide guide and an e-newsletter at www.destination-weddingmag.com.

Event Planning Publications

- *Event Solutions*. Considered the premier national trade magazine for event planners and meeting professionals, *Event Solutions* is a bimonthly publication that covers trends, technologies, and other information of interest to event planners. It's free to qualified professionals and is delivered in print or digital form. To sign up, go to www.event-solutions.com.
- *Expo*. Wedding consultants often find general event planning publications helpful as idea-starters and information wellsprings. *Expo* is useful for wedding consultants because it taps into trade show topics of importance to exhibitors.

Expo is available online free of charge at www.expoweb.com, where you also can read back issues at no charge.

- *Exhibitor magazine.* This publication also serves trade show and event marketing professionals and is available at no charge at www.exhibitoronline.com.

The Advertising Rules of Engagement

What do slogans like "Diamonds are for-
ever," "Fifteen minutes could save you 15% on car insurance," and
"Nothing runs like a Deere" have in common? They're all memorable advertising slogans created to increase awareness and name
recognition for a specific product. And while you don't have to
dream up a catchy tagline or jingle that people will be humming

▲

from coast to coast, you do need to devise a carefully crafted advertising plan that can help boost your business and create a positive image.

Many of the wedding consultants we spoke to rely on word-of-mouth referrals and a proprietary website as the basis of their advertising efforts. Often, these strategies alone are enough to fill a consultant's calendar comfortably. But if you really want to grow your business, you need a well-rounded, multi-pronged marketing program. In this chapter, we'll examine the full range of techniques you can use to market your business and make it the top-of-mind choice for brides who are looking for a creative and responsive wedding consultant.

Smart Tip

Tip...

Always brainstorm a list of goals and expectations for your business before writing a marketing plan. You need to know precisely what you want to achieve with the business, both now and one, three, and five years in the future, before you can identify the marketing strategies that will get you there.

Your Marketing Plan

Before you start dropping dollars on advertising of any kind, it's essential to create a basic marketing plan. This plan doesn't have to be complicated, but it should be detailed enough to serve as a roadmap that keeps your wedding enterprise on track and your marketing efforts on target. In addition, it should be updated periodically as market conditions change so you are always in touch with the needs of your customers.

Your marketing plan can be a part of the business plan you've already written. (Refer to Chapter 4 for information about business plans.) It should describe your target market and the competitive environment you are operating in (this is where your market research comes in—refer to Chapter 3), as well as address how you're going to make your customers aware of your business. Information related to pricing, industry trends, and advertising also has a place in your marketing plan.

SWOT Analysis

An integral part of the marketing plan is the SWOT analysis. This is a strategic planning tool that will help you to identify the internal and external forces that may impact your business, which in turn will help you position your business in a competitive marketplace.

The acronym SWOT stands for:

- *Strengths.* These are the characteristics that make your business special and set it apart from the competition, giving you a competitive advantage. In particular, you'll want to consider what you'll offer that's different or better than that of other wedding planning businesses in your area.
- *Weaknesses.* These are the things you need to overcome or work on that your competitors could take advantage of. These weaknesses can run the gamut from personal traits you need to improve on (such as being a tad too impatient with people who just can't make up their minds or having a tendency to run late),

SWOT Analysis

Here's what a SWOT analysis might look like for a new wedding consultant business that will be operating in a medium-sized market of at least 25,000 people.

Strengths

- ❏ My strong business background (crucial expertise in business development!)
- ❏ My experience with event planning for conventions with 1,000 attendees
- ❏ My strong communication skills (including writing)

Weaknesses

- ❏ No experience with advertising, marketing
- ❏ Can't travel outside of immediate area because of husband's work schedule and child-care needs

Opportunities

- ❏ No other consultants located within five-mile radius
- ❏ New condo community nearly completed is geared toward middle-aged empty nesters that may have marriage-age offspring

Threats

- ❏ Banquet facility at corner of Cleophus Avenue and Ferris has just added a wedding consulting package
- ❏ Rumors that city is changing zoning to disallow homebased businesses

to having a budget that's too slim for a business that hopes to attract wealthy clients.

- *Opportunities.* These are the things you can do that might benefit your business either now or in the future. The idea is to aim high now, then position your business to meet those lofty goals later.
- *Threats.* These include anything that can harm your business, from obstacles like cash-flow problems (common in startup businesses) to stiff competition or a weak local economy.

A SWOT analysis is a simple tool, yet it's used by small businesses and large corporations alike to help them leverage their strengths while identifying things that can derail their company. You'll find that putting these characteristics on paper will give you a provocative snapshot of your business's prospects and serve as a roadmap to help you craft a plan to fulfill them.

Now it's your turn. Try creating your own SWOT analysis using the worksheet provided on the next page. And while you're at it, you should also create a SWOT chart to analyze the strengths and weaknesses of your competition as a way to see how you stack up against them.

Incorporate your completed SWOT analysis into your marketing plan and tuck a copy into your business plan and refer to it often. You'll also want to update the SWOT occasionally as a way to benchmark your successes and identify the new opportunities and threats that lurk around the bend.

Julia Kappel, the wedding consultant in Oak Point, Texas, found out firsthand the benefit of doing a SWOT analysis. "We wrote a formal marketing plan using a SWOT analysis because we wanted to make sure the business was going to be profitable considering that I was going to make it replace my current income and supplement my partner's income," she says. "What we determined from the analysis and market research was that had we done what we originally intended, we would have failed miserably. I can say that with all confidence because there is another consultant doing what we were going to do and she is failing.

"What we learned was that our market area was too small and too far removed from the places where the big money was being spent. We were planning to begin in a small town and move toward Dallas.

> **Smart Tip**
>
> When writing your marketing plan, think about every opportunity you'll have to interact with your customers. These contacts include everything from face-to-face meetings like consultations to email, website marketing efforts, and even the invoices you'll send. Each contact should be considered a potential marketing opportunity.

SWOT Analysis Worksheet

Strengths

1. _____

2. _____

3. _____

Weaknesses

1. _____

2. _____

3. _____

Opportunities

1. _____

2. _____

3. _____

Threats

1. _____

2. _____

3. _____

Instead, we took a little longer to get our ducks in a row and began right in the heart of Dallas."

Tell Them About It

Another important part of your marketing plan is your promotion strategy. Every wedding consultant, from the one-person expert who coordinates just a handful of weddings annually to the consultant who needs a large staff to help handle the workload, must advertise to get new business.

Advertising methods that can prove effective for wedding consultants include word-of-mouth referrals, brochures, business cards, Yellow Pages advertising, and magazine ads. Each of these methods is discussed below. Interactive and social media, both of which are excellent promotional tools, are discussed in Chapter 10, "Cyber Resources."

Word-of-Mouth Referrals

Whoever said there's no such thing as a free lunch must have overlooked word-of-mouth referrals. Not only is the price right—e.g., free—but word-of-mouth praise is one of the most powerful advertising vehicles wedding consultants have at their disposal. One of its major advantages is that you often don't have to do anything special to garner this kind of freebie publicity. All you must do is to perform your job to the best of your ability, and people will talk favorably about you and your willingness to do whatever it takes to satisfy the customer.

"Word-of-mouth is a considerably important means of getting clients," says Robbi Ernst, president and founder of June Wedding Inc. "[Earning such accolades] should be an impetus for wedding consultants to make certain that every wedding they produce is a first-class wedding, no matter how limited the budget is."

Alexander Hiam, author of *Marketing for Dummies* (For Dummies), says the key to getting good word-of-mouth referrals is to influence what your customers say about you. You can do this in a number of ways. Some wedding consultants call their clients a few weeks after the wedding to get feedback and verify their satisfaction. Doing this projects a positive image of you and your company because it's so rare for businesspeople in service industries to follow up after the sale. You might also get a referral or two from the satisfied bride during the conversation, which you can turn into a word-of-mouth opportunity by using her name when you call the person to whom she referred you.

Influencing Word-of-Mouth Referrals

Robbi Ernst, a consulting expert and founder of June Wedding Inc., is a firm believer that word-of-mouth referrals can come from many areas—even the brides who don't use your services.

"I have found through the years that wedding consultants, especially new ones, tend to become impatient when they get phone calls from prospective clients. The attitude seems to be that it is such a nuisance when they get a sense that the caller is 'shopping around' or 'trying to get free advice,'" Ernst says. "I take a different stand. I feel that any time one can do something for someone else, even if the person is not going to hire me because of her financial situation, that I should do so. If nothing else, that bride is more likely to tell someone she had a good experience in talking with me, and what better way to get free advertising? Besides, the alternative to that is for her to tell someone that I was rude or impatient or to say something else negative about my company."

Another way to influence word-of-mouth is by doing something positive and visible in your community or on the wedding business circuit. For example, you could host a complimentary hour-long, do-it-yourself wedding workshop for brides with small budgets and invite the local media to attend. Any coverage you get is bound to focus not only on your benevolence, but also on the services you offer. That can lead to new business.

A third way to influence word-of-mouth is by becoming involved in local business organizations, like Rotary International or the chamber of commerce. As you may know, many people have the perception that wedding consultants are "dabblers," who like to attend weddings and have turned that interest into a little side business. Although thankfully this perception is changing, you can do more to establish yourself as a professional by networking at meetings of these local organizations. The members, in turn, are likely to use your services themselves, or recommend you to others in need of a wedding coordinator.

Brochures

A brochure is a great tool for reaching brides-to-be in the places they're likely to frequent, like bridal shops, bakeries that specialize in wedding cakes, photography studios, caterers, and so on. The cover should prominently feature your company name and have your own, unique logo.

Other elements the brochure should include are:

Smart Tip

Tip...

Always carry a supply of brochures with you so you always have one available to hand out with your business card when any conversation turns to matters matrimonial. Tuck them into an envelope or a protective sleeve to keep them in pristine condition as you travel around.

- A detailed list of your services
- Testimonials from satisfied customers ("ABC Bridal made my wedding a wonderful day to remember!" — Constance Zebracki, Detroit Lakes, Minnesota)

- Contact information (your address, phone number, fax number, email address, website address)

Brochures can take many forms. The most common are the two- and three-panel brochures that, when folded, will fit into a standard No. 10 envelope. Stationery and office supply stores sell brochure stationery and envelopes that can be used in a laser or inkjet printer. But for a more professional look, have your brochures designed by a professional artist and printed on a high-quality paper stock to reflect the high quality your customers can expect from your business.

Your brochure is a powerful marketing tool that works for you day or night, even when you're not there. For this reason, you'll want to distribute it widely. Start by making arrangements with local bridal and florist shops to display your brochure, either for a small fee or a promise to recommend them to the brides who engage your services. Be sure to provide a small literature holder with the brochures to keep them neat and tidy on the counter. (These acrylic racks are available for as little as $3.50 each through office supply stores like OfficeMax and Staples.)

Bright Idea

Create a scannable business card so those who want to save the information and ditch the card can find you again. Use black type on a white background (scanners have trouble reading dark or patterned backgrounds), and choose a simple typeface like Helvetica (no script!). Since logos are hard to scan, make sure your business name also appears in type.

You'll also want to consider mailing your brochure to prospective brides in the geographical area you serve. Many publications sell their mailing lists and can segment the names by ZIP code or other criteria you choose. Refer to Chapter 3 for more information on how to find and purchase mailing lists.

Regional bridal shows often compile their own mailing lists and make them available for sale. These are called "hot lists," or compilations of likely buyers. To purchase a list of bridal show attendees, contact the show's public relations office a few weeks after the show (since this gives them sufficient time to finalize their list). You'll pay a set fee—sometimes as low as $50 to $60—per 1,000 names to use the list once.

Business Cards

Here's a great way to advertise at a very low cost. Your business card is not only your calling card, but it reminds a prospective bride—or her parent(s)—that you're only a phone call or an email away. As a result, you should distribute your card freely wherever you go. The sole exception: Don't ever give out business cards at a wedding you are coordinating, unless you are specifically asked for one. There's nothing less professional or tackier than placing a neat little pile of business cards on the cake table or handing out unsolicited cards to the unmarried guests in attendance.

Business cards should be designed to match your business stationery, and it's generally more cost-effective to print both the stationery and cards at the same time. You should have your cards printed on the highest quality paper stock you can afford to give them a high-end look that will reflect well on your business. Having a high-end look is also the reason why you should avoid printing your own cards on stock you purchase from an office supply store. Business cards are very inexpensive—as little as $50 for 250 full-color cards on high-quality stock—so do-it-yourself printing is verboten for a professional wedding consultant.

The Yellow Pages

In this age of electronic communication, it may seem strange to consider the Yellow Pages to be a viable advertising tool. Yet the wedding consultants who we spoke to said that their Yellow Pages ad was still a low-maintenance, low-cost workhorse that had great value in their advertising mix. To begin with, an ad works for you 24/7. Also, a standard phone directory listing ensures that your business will show up online at sites like Yellowpages.com. Go to www.yellowpages.com now and try typing "wedding planner" into your browser, along with your city. Depending how large your urban area is, you'll get dozens of results that include everything from wedding consultants to DJs, florists, musicians, and more. These online directories also have links that allow the user to email the information to themselves, send it to their smartphone, or share it on Facebook and Twitter.

There are two types of print ads to choose from. The first is the line ad, which is the basic listing that's published under a heading like "Wedding Consultants" or

"Wedding Services." Line ads normally contain only the business name, address, and telephone number, and are provided to you free of charge when you activate your phone service. But do pay whatever additional cost may be necessary to have your website address included in the listing. Brides with smartphones will find this information especially useful and convenient.

The second type of print ad is the display ad. It's usually boxed and is much larger than a line ad. As a result, a display ad can contain far more copy, including details about the services you offer, your hours of operation, your logo, and even a piece

---

Five Biggest Yellow Pages Mistakes

Barbara Koch, author of *Profitable Yellow Pages*, says you can make your display ads more effective by avoiding these common mistakes:

1. *Selling the category, not your business.* If a bride opens the phone book to or accesses the wedding consultant listings online, she doesn't have to be convinced that she should hire a consultant. So sell yourself in your ad to make her choose you over the others who are listed. Emphasize what's special about your business and tell her something she needs to know that sets you apart from your competition.

2. *Selling products, not benefits.* Of course you handle catering, flowers, and other wedding-day services. So instead, emphasize what makes your business special and how in turn you can make the bride's day special.

3. *Emphasizing nothing.* This has more to do with the appearance of the ad than the content. If everything in the ad is visually the same (same typeface, same type size, etc.), nothing seems important. At the very least, use a larger type size for your header, and add color to make the ad stand out.

4. *Using tired phrases.* Terms like "full service," "number one," and "highest quality" are so overused they've lost their meaning. Instead, use action verbs and powerful language, like "making dreams come true," to convey your message.

5. *Using your business name as your header.* Putting your company name at the top of the ad doesn't grab attention or tell the reader anything about your business.

Dollar Stretcher

Always check to see if your competition places display ads. If not, that's a pretty strong indication that it's not necessary to spend the money to attract callers.

of clip art that relates to your business—like a bridal bouquet or a pair of wedding rings. Display ads are sold by the column width and the depth in inches. At one time, display ad costs were very high, but now that there are so many print and electronic directories, prices are more affordable. Let the cost be your guide to whether or not it's worth it to have a display ad.

Often, a line ad is enough to attract calls from interested brides, as Donna Horner, the wedding consultant in Austin, Texas, can attest. She has coordinated nearly 10,000 weddings in a career that has spanned 25 years and does little advertising outside of her line ad. But if you do decide to buy a display ad, examine the directory listings carefully to make sure there's an appropriate category heading that brides can find easily.

You might think that placing a display ad when everyone else has a line ad would be a great way to grab attention. But that's not necessarily the case, according to Barbara Koch, author of *Profitable Yellow Pages*.

"Many small-business owners buy more ad space than they need," Koch says. "Yellow Pages ads are effective because advertisers have a captive audience who have already made a decision to buy. But that's also what makes it unnecessary to buy a display ad in most cases. The real role of your ad is to get the customer to choose you over someone else, and factors like your location may be what actually causes them to call you."

Overall, Yellow Pages advertising is a cost-effective technique for attracting business. But it does have a few disadvantages. For instance, let's say your local directory is published in April, but you didn't start your business until May. A full year will go by before your ad ever appears in the directory. On the other hand, directory assistance callers will be able to request your telephone number, but only if they know the exact name of your business. Luckily, having an online listing in the wedding category will help to direct interested parties to your business, even if it's not yet in the Big Book.

Another disadvantage is that if the name of your business begins with a letter at the end of the alphabet, you'll be at the bottom of the list of wedding consultants. If the list isn't very long, that isn't much cause for concern. But if you're operating in a large city that has many wedding consultants, you could be overlooked by starry-eyed, busy brides.

A third disadvantage is that unless you buy a big display ad, your ad may be placed in the gutter, which is the space formed by the adjoining pages in the book. This can make it harder for customers to find your ad, especially if the directory is large and doesn't lie fully flat when opened. Unfortunately, you have no control over the placement of your ad in the directory. The best you can hope for is that the design of your ad or the use of color will make it stand out.

To place a Yellow Pages ad, or for more information, call the publisher of the directory in which you wish to display.

Magazine Display Ads

In magazine publishing, a 60/40 advertising-to-editorial ratio is considered the Holy Grail, which means there's plenty of room for your paid advertisement in practically any magazine in which you choose to advertise.

It's best to advertise only in consumer publications that cater specifically to brides since, at any given time, only 1 percent of the population is considering marriage. The most widely read publication in the bridal industry is *Brides*, which also offers online advertising in addition to its print publication. In addition, many cities have their own bridal and style magazines, which are excellent vehicles for your ad.

Advertising in these publications can be expensive. To get the best possible rate, run what's known as a schedule of ads, since the per-insertion rate is reduced when you repeat the ad over a set period of time. Another bonus: Studies show that ads that are repeated regularly tend to generate the most interest among consumers. It's really not beneficial to advertise only when you need business, so save your money if you can only afford one or two insertions.

If you have some imagination and access to a publishing software program like Adobe InDesign, you can try your hand at designing your own ad. But since you'll be spending a lot of money running that ad, which has the potential of being seen by thousands of readers, you probably should have it professionally designed. You don't have to go to a big advertising agency to get the job done. It's far more cost-effective to find a freelance artist through your local Yellow Pages, professional advertising association, or university art department. Even the internet can be a viable source. Using a search engine, type in keywords like "commercial artist" or "graphic designer" to locate prospects.

Like your Yellow Pages display ad, your magazine print ad should be eye-catching and informative. Focus on the unique things

Bright Idea

Cinema advertising (the on-screen ads that run before the start of a feature film) is a great place to advertise your services to a local audience. According to OTX Research, 75 percent of moviegoers pay attention to the preshows, so you could reach a lot of prospective customers. For more information, contact the advertising representative at your local cineplex.

your business does best, and be sure to give full contact information, including your telephone number (and toll-free number, if applicable), and your website and email addresses. You should develop a special logo for use in your ad, as well as on your stationery and business cards, and any other marketing materials. It's best not to use a clip-art logo. Chances are, someone else is already using that clip art in his or her advertising. Always go for a custom-designed logo that reflects your personal taste and style.

Incidentally, if your advertising budget is slim, you might try newsletter and website advertising, which usually costs considerably less than advertising in a glossy magazine. Many bridal websites (like www.theknot.com and www.bestweddingsites. com) accept advertising in their newsletters and sell advertising banners right on their websites.

Cyber Resources

You probably already have a personal webpage and a Facebook page. Maybe you follow people with interesting lives on Twitter. Or you're always using your farm cash to "unwither" the crops you neglected on Farmville because you're too busy to plow them. So now it's time to consider the many ways you can use the internet and social networking to establish an online presence and promote your new consulting business (no avatar necessary).

Your Cyber Presence

Well-conceived and executed internet and viral marketing efforts are crucial for aspiring wedding consultants because the audience they serve is so tech-savvy. According to InternetStats.com, 77.3 percent of the U.S. population (which topped 311 million people in 2010) used the internet, while 43 percent of Americans used Facebook in 2010. That equates to nearly 240 million internet users and nearly 134 million Facebook users, respectively. Considering that at any one given time, about 1 percent of the population is in marriage-preparation mode, that's a lot of brides you could reach simply by having a strong and pervasive internet presence.

In this chapter, you'll get the lowdown on the various ways you can use the internet to manage and build your business, including a discussion of the cyber tools no wedding consultant can be without these days: a website, a blog, Facebook, Twitter, LinkedIn, and even YouTube.

Your 24/7 Resource

Brides and grooms aside for a moment, the internet will be an outstanding resource for you, too, for everything from advice on how to handle sticky business matters like collections problems to locating vendors that can provide the myriad services and products your brides will need. You should also spend some time online in the formative days of your business doing preliminary market research, investigating local zoning ordinances and tax implications, looking up the hours and contact information for local reception venues you'll be contacting, and checking out anything else you can think of to make your job easier. Since you might not be ready to purchase professional wedding planning software yet, create some folders on your computer where you can copy and paste all the information you collect so it's handy when you're ready to make some decisions.

You can also find plenty of small-business advice on the internet, starting with the wisdom on the SBA website at www.sba.gov, the IRS at www.irs.gov, and *Entrepreneur* magazine at www.entrepreneur.com. There also are numerous blogs and bulletin boards where wedding professionals and vendors gather virtually to exchange ideas. A couple to explore: The Knot's wedding obsession blog at www.

theknot.com; and digital marketing agency Splendid Communications' blog at www. thinksplendid.com.

And, of course, you can follow your fave wedding sites, like the Association for Wedding Professionals, by becoming a Facebook friend, signing up for RSS feeds, or becoming a follower on Twitter. These sites provide a wealth of information in micro-bites that are perfect for the busy wedding consultant on the go.

But when you're surfing and signing up, just remember the old adage: You get exactly what you pay for. Always consider the source when searching for information, and stick with reliable and reputable companies or people. For instance, if you're looking for help writing your business plan, you know you can trust a source like the SBA, rather than the droll site called "Nick's 12-Step Plan for Making Big Bucks."

Yet another useful purpose for the internet is as a tool to fulfill the bridal party's unusual requests. Does the bride want an Elvis impersonator to serenade her hound dog at the reception? Search on the keywords "celebrity impersonators," plus the name of your city, to see what pops up. Or maybe she remembers seeing charming replicas of 18th century tussy-mussy holders in a magazine years ago and insists on using them for her bridesmaids' bouquets. Type "tussy mussy" into your browser and see where it leads you.

The Wedding Consultant Website

Even though more exciting and interactive networking tools like Facebook and Twitter are grabbing all the attention these days, there's no doubt that a website still should be the centerpiece of a cyber promotion strategy. Obviously, websites can harbor far more information in much more detail than a mere Facebook page or a tiny, 140-character tweet. And of course, information that's available 24/7 is exactly what brides are looking for as they do their due diligence before selecting a wedding consultant and other nuptial-related services. So if you're not out there when they're looking, they definitely will go somewhere else.

"I get a lot of hits on my website, and probably 50 percent of my business comes from those leads," says Packy Boukis, the wedding consultant in Ohio. "It happens because I have links from some very high traffic areas, and I keep track of and update them whenever I make any changes to my website."

"A company website is imperative!" adds Robbi Ernst III of June Wedding Inc. "It is the modern brochure. As a matter of fact, the money that wedding consultants once put into designing and creating a slick, elegant, informative brochure is equivalent to

▲

Important Web Addresses at a Glance

Here are some websites you can use to do business better or find useful (free) advice:

❍ *Amazon*: sells books, CDs, and videos (www.amazon.com)

❍ *Dogpile Web Search:* a web search tool that combines many of the best search engines into one (www.dogpile.com)

❍ *Entrepreneur*: the premier source for small-business advice (www.entrepreneur.com)

❍ *FindLaw*: for legal resources (www.findlaw.com)

❍ *Google Calendar*: a free schedule organizer. All you need is a Google account and password to get started (https://calendar.google.com)

❍ *Hotwire.com*: Hotel and airfare discounter (www.hotwire.com)

❍ *IRS*: premier source for tax tips and advice (www.irs.gov)

❍ *Mapquest*: online driving directions in the United States (www.mapquest.com)

❍ *Memo to Me*: a free internet reminder service (www.memotome.com)

❍ *National Association for the Self-Employed*: offers advice, group insurance, and more (www.nase.org)

❍ *National Association of Enrolled Agents*: a source for locating accountants (www.naea.org)

❍ *National Small Business Network*: interactive resource for home-office and small-business owners (www.businessknowhow.net)

❍ *Picasa*: free software from Google for downloading, editing, and organizing photos (http://picasa.google.com)

❍ *SBA*: the small-business owner's best friend, with extensive FAQs and advice (www.sba.gov)

❍ *Travelocity*: a site for airline and hotel reservations worldwide (www.travelocity.com)

❍ *U.S. Census Bureau*: the official government website for statistics and demographics (www.census.gov)

❍ *ZIP code look-up*: helps you find any ZIP code in the United States and its possessions (www.usps.com)

what one must put into the designing and creating of a slick, elegant, and informative website."

An insightful, easily navigable website is really important if you live and work in a city that is a known tourist destination. Destination weddings are big business, with couples traveling to romantic tropical locales like Hawaii or cosmopolitan cities like New York for their nuptials. Disney World is another hot spot for weddings, and the resort capitalizes on this by offering its own wedding packages. So if you are willing to handle long-distance arrangements (which is a breeze, thanks to technology), you need to get that website up as soon as possible.

The Basics of Web Design

Because your website is virtual advertising that's available on demand 24 hours per day, it's important to spend a fair amount of time considering what it should say. Before approaching a website designer, consider the questions you think your customers would have when searching for a wedding consultant. Here are examples of the kinds of questions they might have:

- How can I set up a reasonable budget?
- What is the average amount I can expect to spend on my entire wedding?
- Can you plan my entire wedding?
- How can you help me on my wedding day?
- Can you coordinate my honeymoon arrangements?
- Can you help me find a good florist (or caterer or DJ or baker)?
- Can we correspond by text or email, or must we always meet in person?
- Is there a charge for the initial consultation?
- What do your services cost?
- How will I pay you? Do you have a payment plan?
- Do you have references?
- How can I reach you?

Armed with these questions, you should next consider how you want the site to look. You want it to be user-friendly, yet elegant so it reflects the tastes of your customers. You can do this by keeping the web page design clean and uncluttered, and the copy succinct. This doesn't mean you can't say what you need to say. But you don't have to

Dollar Stretcher

It's not necessary to include wedding package prices on your website. It's always better to hook brides with photos and descriptions of the romantic, elegant affairs you can help to create as a way to entice them to call for more details about fees.

tell readers every detail related to your business. You just want them to have enough information to make an informed decision about whether hiring you would be a good idea, and whether doing so will fit well in their plans—and their budgets.

To get some inspiration and ideas for your site, spend some time perusing the sites of other wedding consultants, particularly those in your market area. The idea here isn't to crib any ideas or copy another consultant's winning design, but to get a sense of what appeals to you and what type of look you'd like for your own website. Armed with this information (and the URLs), you then can make an appointment to meet with a web designer to get the process rolling.

It's always preferable to hire a web designer to create your site than to try to go it alone. While there is undeniably good software available to help you build a website yourself (Adobe Dreamweaver CS5 comes to mind), as well as affordable template-based software (such as Intuit Website-Building Software), chances are, your talents lie in other areas (say, wedding planning). Your site is a representation of who you are, what you represent, and what types of services you provide, so you want it to be elegant, informative, and easy to navigate. Unless you were a web designer in a previous life, you really need to leave the job to the pros.

And whatever you do, don't use the personal web space provided by your ISP, even as a temporary, stopgap measure. The address alone will give away the fact that not a lot of thought went into this very important marketing tool, not to mention that a whole boxful of other people may be using a website with a similar look to yours. This is also why you should avoid templated websites of any kind. Imagine using the same website template as a parent who posts her baby's teething pictures, a gun-and-knife show promoter, or a Goth teen who's into creepy piercings. You get the idea.

"The truth is, most people don't have the technical skills or the time to produce a good website," says Fred Elbel, owner of Elbel Consulting Services in Lakewood, Colorado. "Your website is an extension of your marketing plan and has to be a notch above your competition, plus optimizing a website for success is an art and a science. Most people don't have the skill or time to do all that."

Depending on the number of pages on your site, you can expect to pay anywhere from $1,000 to $3,500 for a professionally designed website. Photos will drive up the cost further. However, don't skimp on photos to save a few bucks. The best way to sell brides on your services is to show them pictures that represent what you can

Tip...

Smart Tip

Word has a four-page "Web Site Creation Strategy" form in its template database that you might find helpful when you're considering what information to include on your website. Even if you don't use Word, you can download the template for free at http://office.microsoft.com/en-us/templates/.

do, from interacting with radiant brides to creating stunning reception rooms. Initially, you'll have to use stock photos on your site, but eventually you'll be able to replace those images with photos right from the weddings you coordinated under the aegis of your new business.

You can find many web designer leads by Googling the term and the name of your city. However, to be sure you find someone skillful, reliable, and reputable, ask your business acquaintances and friends who already have websites you like (bridal-related or not) for a recommendation. Business organizations to which you belong also may be able to direct you to vetted professionals.

Before meeting with your web designer, create and finalize the copy you'd like to use. The copy should be concise and not too flowery—an excess number of adjectives will make you sound like an amateur instead of a romantic. In addition, keep the copy brief so each page runs no more than a screen or two. Many people find it annoying to have to keep scrolling down as they read, and even the most starry-eyed bride may abandon your site if there's too much to read.

If you don't feel up to the task of writing scintillating, crisp website copy yourself (and there is a knack to it), hire a freelance writer to do it for you. Visit a site like MediaBistro.com or Google "freelance web copy" or "SEO content writer" for leads. You also can get leads from your local chamber of commerce or other business organizations.

Building Your Website

The next decision you must make relates to the type of website you want to build. A simple option is the online business card, which is no more than a single screen that gives your company name and contact information, like your address, phone number, and fax number. This type of website is actually quite easy to build, even for those who don't know a byte from a baud, and is useful as a cyber "placeholder" until you can have a professional site built. However, the disadvantage of this kind of web page is that there's not much room for information. Since you're likely to have a lot to say (and a sales pitch to make), don't leave a business card site up long; launch your fully developed site as soon as possible.

Here are the basic elements (i.e., pages) that you're likely to need on your new wedding website:

- *Welcome (home) page.* Since this is the first page a bride or her entourage see, the welcome page should succinctly describe the services you offer, from complete wedding coordination to "blueprint" packages. The operative word here is "succinct." At this point, you just want to introduce the reader to your services, not overwhelm her with details. All you need on this page is a navigation bar near or across the top with links to more detailed information (the links are discussed in detail below). Alternatively, you can have an elegant home page that consists only of links and photos underscored by music rather than text. Just keep in mind that you have only a couple of seconds to grab the attention of visitors, so make sure a text-free home page is a real attention-getter.

- *List of services.* Here's where you'll include detailed information about your services. You'll need to provide enough details about the scope of your services so brides will know exactly how you can help them. It's usually advisable to include a detailed list of what is included with each wedding package, from full coordination to wedding-day only coordination and consulting. This is where the most persuasive selling needs to be done to entice brides to contact you, so make sure you spend a fair amount of time planning what the page should say and how the information should be presented.

- *Your credentials/experience.* This information is usually parked under the "About" link and presents both your background and the reasons why you're qualified to coordinate weddings. If you don't have any prior wedding consulting experience, no worries—focus instead on the depth of your service network and any experience you have from industries that may translate to your new profession. This might include anything from an interior design background (which is just as detail-oriented as wedding planning) to corporate busi-

Bright Idea

Writing a personal letter to brides for the "About" page is a clever way to introduce yourself without revealing that you're new to wedding planning. Talk about how much helping brides means to you or your attention to detail. You can even admit that you're a romantic. It's a simple, heartfelt way to make a connection with brides.

ness experience (where you certainly have to be well-organized and efficient). Obviously, you won't want to state that you haven't been in business very long, so instead focus on your commitment to brides, your commitment to the community, and anything else that makes you sound solid and reliable. After you've coordinated a few weddings, you can rewrite this information to focus on your actual experience.

Always include credentials like university degrees or certifications on your About page. If the degree you've earned is too far afield of the wedding industry (say, industrial engineering or nuclear physics), leave off the major and just list the degree (such as Bachelor of Arts) and the name of the university or college.

- *Photos.* Until you have actually coordinated some weddings and have permission to use the photos, you'll have to populate your website with stock photos, which are photographs that are licensed for use so you don't have to hire a photographer, although you will have to pay a fee to a stock art company. You'll want to select photos of happy brides on the arm of their new husbands, people enjoying themselves at sumptuous receptions, dancing, and other wedding-day moments. Eventually you'll be able to use photos from actual weddings you've coordinated, but always ask for permission to use them before posting them. It's always a good idea to have anyone in the photos sign a model release so you have proof in writing that they agreed. You'll find a simple model release you can use on page 114, although you might want to run it by your attorney to make sure it protects you adequately. Additionally, Microsoft has a free release form template at its site at http://office.Microsoft.com. Search on "Release form for use of one's image" to be directed to the template.

- *Testimonials.* Once you start coordinating weddings and wowing clients with your professionalism, you're likely to start getting thank-you text messages, emails, or letters from grateful brides, parents, and others in the wedding party. Start collecting these messages so you can use brief excerpts on your website, along with the name of the satisfied customer. But as with photographs, obtain permission to reprint these messages and the name of the sender on your website so there are no misunderstandings later.

- *Resources.* Include links to wedding industry-related information that the reader might find helpful. Far from giving away "trade secrets," offering such links shows that you care about the reader and want to help her as much as possible with the planning of her big day. A couple of consumer-oriented wedding sites to include are The Knot (www.theknot.com) and the Wedding Channel (www. weddingchannel.com). Some sites even offer reciprocal links when you link to them, meaning they'll return the favor and include a link to your site on their site.

- *Package prices details.* Publishing fees online where anyone—including your competition—can see them is a matter of personal preference. It's certainly convenient for brides who are still shopping around, but you lose the opportunity to sell a bride on the depth and breadth of your services if she perceives that the cost is prohibitive before ever speaking to you. On the other hand, divulging package prices can help to cut down on calls or emails from indecisive "lookie-loos." Because you usually don't want brides to compare you to the competition on the basis of price alone, you might want to categorize your services and packages using terms like "best value" or "most exclusive," and let the reader draw her own conclusions.

- *Contact.* Provide full contact information and the hours during which you can be reached. If you work out of a home office or you never meet brides there, you should keep your home address private from the general public. Be sure to include your phone number(s) for calls and texts, as well as your email address. It's also a good idea to have a fill-in-the-blank form on your website for information and/or quote inquiries that the reader can fill out and send. Finally, in addition to having a "Contact us" link on your navigation bar, make sure your contact information appears at the bottom of every linked page on your site so readers can find it easily.

- *RSS feed.* Add an RSS ("Really Simple Syndication") feed to your website to send syndicated text (including blog entries), audio, and video about the bridal industry directly to those who visit your website. In a way it's like having your own personal wire service. Use it as a way to keep subscribers constantly updated about what you're doing. For instance, an RSS feed can be used to send out news releases about your business, which could result in free media coverage for your business if they're picked up by a journalist. Or send out information about your services to keep potential customers informed even if they're not yet ready to book with you. You may find it's premature to include an RSS feed on your website when you first start your business, but keep it in mind for the future.

- *Other links.* Press mentions (e.g., positive comments in the media that position you as a wedding expert and your company as a fabulous service provider) should be included as you acquire them. Also, a list of frequently asked questions makes a useful addition to a wedding business website.

> **Tip...**
>
> **Smart Tip**
> It's absolutely essential that you keep your website updated with fresh information and photos. This will keep brides coming back to see what's new and exciting on your site. Also, if you launch a blog, make time to post new entries regularly. If you can't keep up with the task, or you don't have much to say, don't launch it.

You should expect to work closely with your designer to make decisions about copy placement, colors, typefaces, and so on. Don't just dump the project into his or her lap. The website should reflect your style and taste, so you should be involved in all stages of its development. But do rely on the designer's best judgment when it comes to level of interactivity, navigation tools, and artwork.

Name That Domain

Once your website is fully developed and operational, your next task is to select and register a unique domain name. If you're lucky, you'll be able to use the business name you've already selected for your business as your domain name. But if by chance your chosen name has already been registered, you should have a few names ready in reserve. In any event, it's probably best to include the word "weddings" in your name, as in "everafterweddings.com," and "Designmywedding.com," both of which are being used by wedding consultants interviewed for this book.

There are many companies that can register your domain name. Two of the best known these days are www.domain.com and www.godaddy.com, but you can find many more, all of which are competitively priced, by Googling "domain names." Your computer consultant also should be able to recommend a reputable domain provider. You can expect to pay about $12 for a one-year registration, although it's not uncommon for GoDaddy and some

> ## Fun Fact
>
> One of the earliest domain name providers, www.domain.com, pretty much had a lock on the entire industry and used to charge $70 to register a domain name for a period of two years. Intense competition from other companies has caused the cost of domain registration to drop to as little as $5 a year.

of the others to offer domains on a limited time basis for as little as $5.99 a year. Once you register that name, it's yours forever, as long as you keep paying the annual registration fee.

Your Web Host

You're now just one step away from having a live website. The final step is to select a web host site where your site will reside so users can access it 24 hours a day. Examples of well-known web hosts include EarthLink Web Hosting, Yahoo! Small Business, and Host Monster. In addition, domain name providers (including GoDaddy) usually are web hosts, too, so you'll have many companies from which to choose. However, it's advisable to stay away from extremely small or new web hosts. When a web host doesn't have a prior track record, you'll have no idea how reliable it is, whether it goes down very often, or whether its customer service department is prompt and responsive.

The price of web fame is quite modest—often as low as $4.99 a month for 10GB of space, or $7.99 a month for 150GB of space. GoDaddy, which is apparently trying to corner the market on web hosting and domain names, offers hosting for as low as $2.99 a month with a 36-month contract.

You'll find a list of reliable domain name providers and web hosts in the Appendix.

Keywords

As you probably know, people searching the internet aren't magically directed to your site—they get there because you've embedded specific search engine keywords into your website. These are the words people use in a browser to find specific information, products, or services. Your keywords need to be specific enough so they'll turn up in searches, but not so obscure or focused that they may not occur to those who are searching. At the same time, keywords shouldn't be so general that they yield too many hits, since this will cause your site to rank low on the results list.

Keywords are placed right into the text of your website. Here's a list of basic keywords that might be appropriate for a wedding consultant: wedding planner, wedding consultant, wedding coordinator, wedding planner consultant, wedding coordination, bridal consultant, wedding planner + the name of your city, event management, event planner destination wedding.

Another way to increase the chances that brides will land right at your cyber door is by using pay-per-click (PPC) advertising. PPC ads are the clickable links that appear on search engine pages whenever someone searches for information, such as "wedding planner Ft. Wayne." Each time someone clicks on the link, the person is taken directly to the advertiser's (your) website, which is known as a click-through, and the advertiser (you again) pays for that hit. The hope is that these click-throughs will result in business for your company, although the reality is that the conversion rate of "click to

> **Tip...**
>
> **Smart Tip**
> With more than 15 billion websites worldwide, you have to work hard to be seen. So pick your keywords carefully, then use a keywords tracker tool like Wordtracker.com to gauge their effectiveness. Pick top keywords to be among the top searches and low-demand keywords to minimize the number of pages returned so your page comes up higher in searches.

order" is very low—about 2 percent, according to Google AdWords, and as low as .05 percent, according to other internet sources.

Still, it's a good idea to at least try PPC advertising because at the very least, you know that those who are doing the clicking are in the mood to buy. In addition, PPC advertising tends to be inexpensive. For example, Google AdWords (discussed below) charges $0.01 per click.

The PPC market has pretty much been cornered by Google AdWords (Adwords. Google.com), Yahoo! Search Marketing (www.searchmarketing.yahoo.com), and Microsoft adCenter (https://adcenter.microsoft.com/), and you don't just automatically secure your coveted keywords by handing over your credit card number. You actually have to bid on them, which can drive the cost up—way up—if you choose keywords that are in high demand. Still, PPC deserves a look, even if your advertising budget is relatively modest.

Google AdWords

One PPC keyword advertising company to check out is Google AdWords. AdWords ads pop up under a "Sponsored Links" banner in the side column of a search page (usually along the right side of the screen). As with other PPCs, your ad appears when someone searches on Google using the keywords you have imbedded in your website. This is beneficial because, as Google puts it, "you'll be advertising to an audience that's already interested in your business."

AdWords are also customizable. For example, you can confine your ads to a certain geographical area, set a daily budget for the number of clicks, and update or change your keywords list any time you wish.

There's no minimum monthly charge to use AdWords after a $5 activation fee. Other fees include a $0.01 cost-per-click fee (with a minimum cost-per-thousand impressions of $.025), and a minimum payment of $10 for prepaid accounts. You can choose a prepay or post-pay option using a major credit card. For more information or to take a short online instructional course, go to www.adwords.google.com.

Social Networking and Other Viral Marketing Tools

Websites are a really important part of a company's advertising mix, but these days, savvy marketers also have to use every social networking and viral marketing tool available to reach their audience. Here are the top tools to consider:

Facebook

Facebook (www.facebook.com) has been transformed from its origins as a social network for college students into a viable networking and branding tool. Use Facebook to literally put a face on your business—post your own photo, wedding photos, and anything else that might be of interest to brides. For that matter, you should create two separate Facebook pages: a personal page for yourself, with your profile and picture, and a business page for your consultancy.

"Facebook allows you to get your brand out to a wide audience base in a short time," says Jason Brown, a Michigan public relations consultant. "When I heard that in terms of size Facebook is the seventh largest "country" in the world, that hit home for me. It helped me spread the word about my company, goals, and objectives a lot faster than if I hadn't used web channels."

Be sure to put the Facebook logo on your website so people can "friend" you and keep up with what's new and exciting in your business and the world of matters matrimonial.

Twitter

Who would believe that 140-character messages could carry so much clout? Yet that's the power of Twitter (www.twitter.com), a hot micro blogging tool used to send messages, or "tweets," to anyone who subscribes. You can use it to update your brides on new services you're offering, to inform them about a show they should attend, or share myriad other details about the industry and your business. But above all, Twitter is used to keep your business top-of-mind for brides who have engaged your services, as well as others who are still just looking.

"Twitter has really changed the way of doing business, particularly for small businesses," Brown says. "When just starting out in business, you don't have a lot of advertising/marketing dollars to spend to find your customer base. Social media outlets like Twitter give you that opportunity to interact with new customers, and all it costs you is time."

Brown stresses that the only way Twitter works for small-business owners is if you engage your followers rather than trying to sell to them. "It's OK to throw in an offer now and then, but for the most part it's important to educate followers on what value you bring to the table," he says. "If you can do that, then there's a better chance they will become your customer."

Even though Twitter is great for small businesses, save your tweets for when you have something important to say. Sending a tweet too frequently is like crying "Wolf!" too often—the messages lose their impact.

Blogs

These personal online journals are usually linked to an existing website, or are stand-alone vehicles that exist in cyberspace. Blogs also can be delivered via an RSS feed. Use your blog to comment on the state of the industry, cool wedding projects you've encountered, wedding books you've read, or anything else that would interest a bride and her entourage. Just be sure to make the commitment to update it frequently—at least two to three times a week. Otherwise, your blog will go cold and your readers will drop off.

LinkedIn

This business-oriented social networking website was launched in 2003 to encourage professional networking. It now has 40 million members in 170 industries. LinkedIn (www.linkedin.com) is useful for establishing new contacts, reconnecting with old business acquaintances and friends, and finding new business.

So many viral tools, so little time—or not. Social and viral marketing is an integral part of marketing efforts today, so you'd be remiss to overlook any of them. "You need to have your name out there on as many service networks as possible," says Brown, who has the logos of three social networks on his website. "Once you see how they work out, you can focus on just two or three."

Sample Model Release

MODEL RELEASE

By signing this form I give unrestricted permission to _____ to use, display, publish, and otherwise distribute photographs of me (or photos in which I appear) that are in print, digital, or other forms. I release _____ from any and all claims arising from such use.

This agreement is governed by the laws of the state of _____ and represents the entire agreement.

Printed name: _____

Address: _____

Signature: _____ Date: _____

Generating Positive Press

In the past two chapters, you read about the various tried-and-true techniques you can use to spread the word about your business. But of course, advertising and websites, and basically everything else you'll want to try, can add up to some serious cash—cash that may be in short supply when you first start your bridal business.

Fortunately, there are many low-cost public relations tools you can use to generate positive publicity for your business. Among these tools are news releases, feature articles, newsletters, Facebook, Twitter, bridal shows, and networking. Here's a rundown of what they entail and how they can help you.

News Releases

Bright Idea
Set up a separate email address through your ISP just for sending out news releases. That way, you can see quickly whether an editor has responded to your pitch, or whether your email bounced unexpectedly. Add an identifier like "press" to your regular email name so recipients know who's sending the message.

News releases (also called press releases) are like little advertisements for your business. But they're subtler than ads, and in some ways more credible to the reader because when they appear in print they look like news stories rather than advertisements. To appreciate the difference between the two, think of a 30-second TV commercial touting a popular sports drink and a longer infomercial lauding the benefits of a new exercise machine. An infomercial has the appearance of being a news program even though there's a sales pitch at the end. That's the same impact a well-written news release can have.

News releases differ from ads in another important way: There is no cost to run your releases in newspapers, magazines, or other print sources. But there's also no guarantee that what you write will ever appear in print. That's because editors sometimes use news releases as "idea starters" that can be developed into related or more detailed stories. They also use releases as filler material or when they have room on a page with editorial content relating to the same topic you've written about. In that case, the editor usually will use just a smidgeon or a paragraph of what you've written rather than the entire release. But any free publicity is good publicity, so rejoice even if your carefully crafted news release is reduced to just a few lines.

Bright Idea
Packaging a paper news release in a novel way (like sending it rolled up in a champagne flute or securing it with a lacy garter) will definitely spark an editor's interest. Save this technique for really special news, like when announcing your business launch, or if you've been hired to coordinate a celebrity or other important wedding.

Even though it's not a given that your news releases will be picked up at all, you should still send them out faithfully and regularly. News releases are one of the most economical ways you have to promote your business, and a steady stream of releases sent to a publication will increase the chances that at least some of them will appear in print.

The news outlets that are most likely to use news releases about your bridal business are newspapers, magazines, and business publications. If you have a local talk radio station or cable TV station, you might want to put those media outlets on your news release list, too.

The first news release you should write will announce the opening of your new wedding consultant business (see example on page 118). But you can write a news release about nearly anything newsworthy that relates to your business, including:

(see example on page 118)

Smart Tip

Tip...

Always Google or call to find out the name of the person who would be most likely to use your news release. Releases sent to a publication's general email box or mailed to "Editor" or just the name of the publication are far less likely to get into print because they're easily misdirected.

- New services you're offering
- A move to a new location
- An expanded service area, such as a new focus on destination weddings
- Special discounts (e.g., discounts for weddings in the off-season)
- Addition of new staff members
- Your wedding consultant certification
- Special events or seasonal information (such as Valentine's Day packages)

You can also write what's known as a "backgrounder," or a news release that gives general information about your services, hours of operation, and contact information. Be sure to include biographical information about yourself (like educational background and pertinent experience) that emphasizes your qualifications. The hope is that an editor's interest will be piqued by the details about your business, and he or she will want to interview you further for a feature story.

Writing the Release

A good news release will answer the journalists' "w.h." words: who, what, where, when, why, and how. Write a title (headline) for the release that captures the flavor of the release, then put the most important information—usually "who" and "what"—first in the body of the release, since editors tend to cut copy from the end of a release if it's too long to run in its entirety. But more importantly, keep the release short and to the point. It should be no longer than two one-and-a-half or double-spaced pages, at the very most. If the release does flow to a second page, use the word "more" at the

Wedding Consultant News Release

NEWS RELEASE

For Immediate Release

Date: March 8, 20xx

Media Contact: Bonnie Stephens

Telephone: (541) 555-0197

Wedding Consultant Makes Matrimony Into an Art Form

BOISE, IDAHO—Bonnie Stephens is weeping copiously into a soggy tissue for the second time this week. But weddings always have that effect on her, so this certified wedding consultant good-naturedly sees the tears as part of her job.

"I always get a little misty-eyed when one of 'my' brides walks down the aisle," Stephens says. "We work together so closely to plan her special day that I can't help being just as happy and proud as she is."

Stephens is the owner and founder of A Vision in White, a wedding consultant business based in Boise. Her task is to coordinate the seemingly insurmountable mountain of details that go into planning the perfect wedding, from securing the banquet hall to picking the menu, ordering the flowers, coordinating the newlyweds' hotel reservations, and handling everything else in between.

"And of course, the real trick is to get everything to come together correctly and on time," she says with a laugh. "Brides love turning over all those details to me."

Bridal industry statistics show that more and more women are relying on wedding consultants to coordinate the wedding of their dreams. And no wonder. Stephens earns each client's trust by consulting with the bride every step of the way to ensure her satisfaction. She offers numerous wedding coordination packages, including full-service coordination, wedding-day direction, and event planning for the do-it-yourselfer. For a consultation appointment, call A Vision in White at (541) 555-0197.

# # #

bottom of page one to indicate it continues. Use three pound symbols (# # #) to indicate the end of the release.

To alert editors that what they're reading is a news release, use the format shown in the sample release on page 118. Some of the elements this format includes are:

Stat Fact
Ninety percent of news releases never get into print—often because they're incomplete, late, or full of errors. To increase the likelihood that an editor will print your release, check it carefully for typos, time it to arrive while the news is still fresh, provide interesting details that will catch the editor's interest, and include a photo whenever possible.

- *Release information.* Unless your release shouldn't be published right away, it will always say "For Immediate Release" at the top.
- *Contact name.* Your name, email, and phone number go here so editors can call you for further information, if needed.
- *Headline.* This is a succinct description of what the release is about. Center this line over the text of the release. Using bold type will make the headline stand out.
- *Dateline.* This is the city from which the release originates. For example, if your business is located in metropolitan Seattle, the first word before the start of the release text begins should be "SEATTLE," in uppercase type.
- *Text.* This is the body of the release with all the pertinent details, including the journalists' "wh" words (who, what, when, where, why, how).

You don't have to be a journalist to write news releases, although proficiency with the English language is a must (especially a working mastery of grammar and punctuation). But if writing is not your strong suit, consider using a freelance public relations writer to write them for you. Writing rates vary, but you can expect to pay $50 to $150 for a one-page news release (the rate depends on the writer's experience and the geographical area he or she serves). You can find freelance writers through websites like www.mediabistro.com, as well as organizations like the American Society of Journalists and Authors (www.asja.com), the Yellow Pages, local advertising associations, and university journalism departments. You could also use a public relations firm. But most firms work on retainer, and that can be pretty expensive for a new business owner.

Producing the Release

Once you've finalized your copy, you're ready to send your news release out to the media outlets on your mailing list. In most cases, editors prefer to receive news

▲

Making an Impression

Not every news release makes it into print, but sheer volume can make an indelible impression on an editor. Robbi Ernst III of June Wedding Inc. found this out firsthand back in the day when he scored a plum interview with the now-defunct *Modern Bride* magazine.

"When a writer called to interview me for an article about wedding consultants, I asked, 'How did you find me?' " Ernst says. "She replied, 'When I was assigned to write this article, I went to our files and found yours. It's 7 inches thick—full of press releases, articles, and more. I figured that you must know what you are doing, and that's the reason I called." That's a great testimonial to the power of persistence—and best of all, that article in *Modern Bride*, which was published in 1987, brought Ernst his first half-million-dollar client.

Of course, these days there is little likelihood that those paper background files exist—rather, they've probably been digitized for inclusion in the media outlets' proprietary database. So now, you have to dazzle editors and remind them you're around by emailing them frequently. Just be sure you have actual news to impart, and keep it coming regularly to stay in editors' crosshairs.

---

releases via email. So prepare for your media blitz by compiling a list of media outlets that might be interested in receiving your releases, including local newspapers, TV stations, radio stations, and local cable stations. In addition to Googling to find the names and contact information for the editors who are most likely to use your releases, you can find media listings on www.mondotimes.com (where for a fee you can create your own online media list for future use). In addition, FinderBinder (www.finderbinder.com) publishes media directories for 12 major media markets, which you may be able to find in your local library.

When you're ready to send the release, write an attention-getting subject line. Resist the temptation simply to tell in ten words or less what the release is about. Instead, pique the interest of the reader to induce him or her to open the email. To get an idea of how to do this, read the headlines on your local newspaper and observe how copy editors grab readers' attention in just a few words. Then when writing your own subject lines, try to be just as creative and show the reader what the release is about. This is crucial because these days, if a subject line doesn't catch an editor's attention, a release doesn't have a chance of being read.

Since editors may not wish to open attachments, copy and paste the news release into the body of the email. Be sure to preserve the news release header information when pasting the release in. You also should attach the release, preferably in pdf form, to the email, as well as anything else that might be useful to the editor, such as photos.

Some editors still prefer to receive news releases by mail. To meet their needs, print the release on your company letterhead using a high-quality laser or ink jet printer. Standard size (8.5-by-11) white bond paper is preferred. If the release runs to a second page, staple the pages together. Then mail the finished releases in your company's imprinted No. 10 envelopes for the most professional look.

> **Tip...**
>
> ### Smart Tip
>
> The first time you email a news release to an editor, be sure to ask whether he or she would prefer to receive future releases electronically or by snail mail. A printed and mailed release will appeal to people who don't like to scroll while reading, and offering this option could help you score more media face time.

Don't Stop There—Following Up

Your job isn't finished once the emails have been sent or the envelopes are stamped and in the mail. About a week after the releases have been sent, email or call each editor personally. In addition to introducing yourself, politely ask whether he or she has received your release and whether it's likely to be published. Be sure to ask, too, if there are specific types of information he or she is more likely to use. Make a note of these preferences so you can refer to them the next time you're drafting a release.

Feature Articles

Like news releases, feature stories are an excellent way to garner publicity for your business. What makes these articles such powerful and effective tools is the fact that they can be used to position you as an authority in your field. This is a great way to gain credibility in your field while building a solid reputation as a savvy businessperson.

Feature stories can run the gamut from informational articles and how-tos to profiles about your services. The slant you take depends on the type of publication you're planning to send them to. For instance, a story on "The Top 10 Reasons to Hire a Wedding Consultant" might be perfect for the features section of your daily newspaper. On the other hand, an article about your entrepreneurial talents, or your successful business startup, might be more appropriate for the business section of your paper or a specialty business magazine.

Don't overlook the value of sharing your knowledge and insight with readers. The idea is to "wow" them with your creative ideas so they immediately think of you when they're ready to engage someone to coordinate their wedding celebration. So write articles giving tips for creating a beautiful wedding. Share stories about wedding disasters and how they can be averted or fixed. Report on the spectacular wedding you coordinated for the daughter of a leading citizen in your town. Or share information on the season's latest trends and color choices for the bridal party. The possibilities are endless.

Although feature articles can run anywhere from 500 to 2,500 words, depending on the publication, a reasonable length for you to shoot for is 1,000 to 1,500 words. As with news releases, you can use a freelance writer to "ghostwrite," or produce the articles under your byline. You can expect to pay a freelance ghostwriter from $100 to $750 for a 1,200-word article.

Submitting Your Manuscript

As with news releases, most editors prefer to receive feature articles via email. Articles generally should be sent as a Word document in an attachment to the email, since editors will probably edit your electronic document. A catchy subject line, a brief message stating why the article is timely and of interest to the reader, and full contact information also should be included. A few days after emailing the article, follow up by phone with the editor as described earlier to increase the chances that the article will be published.

Always remember to give information about how and where you can be reached.

Beware!

Be sure to submit feature articles to just one editor at a time. Editors generally assume that they're getting an exclusive when you submit an article, and they'll be more than miffed if they discover the article you pitched is appearing in another publication simultaneously. If you find the editor isn't interested, you can submit the article elsewhere.

Newsletters

If you're like most people, your mailbox is probably overflowing with newsletters from everyone from your state senator to your local nursery. There is a good reason for the proliferation of these pithy little news vehicles. They're inexpensive to produce, they're easy to create, and they're a very effective way to spread the news about any product or service you offer.

The main reason you'll want to produce a newsletter is to "upsell," or suggest other fee-generating ways you can help the bride. Say, for example, you've accepted a consulting job that consists of coordinating wedding day basics only, such as arranging for the church, setting up the reception, hiring a disc jockey, and reserving a limousine. You might be able to generate additional work—and income—by sending a newsletter with articles focusing on your honeymoon planning services, tuxedo pick-up and delivery services, and so on. You could also include checklists (such as "Things to Do One Month Before the Wedding") and useful information about things like wedding software and marriage traditions.

You don't have to send a lot of newsletters to get the bride's attention. Rather, to keep the newsletter process manageable, plan on creating a single "stock" newsletter, or a generic piece that can be mailed to each new client as she engages your services. Time the delivery of the newsletter for a couple of weeks after the consultation as a way to jog the bride's memory about the many ways you can help. Put your fee schedule and the lead time you need to complete additional projects right in the newsletter.

The newsletter itself should be written in a concise, journalistic style, no matter whether the intent of its articles is to inform or solicit business. If you feel up to the task, you can use a template-based desktop publishing program to create the newsletter yourself. Word has a number of free templates available at no charge (www.office.microsoft.com), but keep in mind that anyone and everyone can use the same templates. It's usually better to use a program that allows you to create a more individualized look for your business. Other software programs you can investigate include Design & Print Business Edition ($40), Print Shop Professional ($90), and Microsoft Publisher ($140). And of course, you can have a freelance designer create your newsletter for you. To keep the cost down, ask him or her to create a template you can update and change yourself in the future.

The standard size for a newsletter is 8.5 by 11 inches, and it's usually produced in multiples of four pages (although two pages—one sheet with type on the front and back—is also appropriate and easy to produce). In addition, it's perfectly fine to design your newsletter with all words and no artwork to make it easier to email or print. Just make sure the final product isn't too copy-heavy—most people prefer short and succinct over lengthy and wordy.

An 8.5-by-11-inch newsletter of no more than four pages (one sheet folded) will easily fit into a standard business envelope, which is the easiest way to mail it. If you email the newsletter, be sure to ask your

Bright Idea

Consider including a special offer in the newsletter—perhaps a discount on the initial consultation. This will help you to track how many people are reading and using your newsletter.

brides for permission to send them over the months you'll work together. Otherwise, it's spam, no matter how useful the information is.

Bridal Shows

For sheer numbers, there may be no better place to gain quick exposure for your business than a bridal show. These events attract hundreds, or even thousands, of brides-to-be—women who will definitely be consumers of the services you offer.

Bridal shows are generally held in convention centers in large cities. For a fairly reasonable price (anywhere from $600 to $1,300, on average), you can rent booth space in these shows. Then it's up to you to chat up prospective customers, cheerfully hand out your business card and brochure, and otherwise lay the groundwork that will result in new business.

Although it's possible to make a professional impression using just the 10- or 12-foot skirted table that's usually provided with your space, you can also personalize your display area. Since you'll be competing with other companies that offer the same kinds of products and services, strive to be innovative. Use a dressmaker's mannequin to display a lovely vintage wedding gown. Artfully display large photographs of weddings you've coordinated on lace-festooned easels. Or invest in a pre-fab booth that can be set up quickly right in your space. These 10-foot pop-up booths have a steel skeleton that's covered with fabric panels that can support signage, photographs, and other visuals. This kind of display is set up at the back of your booth as a backdrop. There's a wide variety of styles to choose from, including single-unit panels with custom designs or triple units. The multi-unit displays usually require lighting to give them pizzazz.

These booths are easy to assemble and tear down. But while such booths are very eye-catching, they can start at around $600 for the single-panel model and run up into the stratosphere. They also don't usually include the graphics, which you'll need to have created separately by a graphic designer. The halogen lights recommended for these displays start at about $35 each. You'll find a few trade show booth distributors listed in the Appendix.

Smart Tip

Tip...

Don't just exchange pleasantries and business cards when you network at professional business organization meetings. Plan a follow-up meeting with people whose interests mesh with yours, or those who might even be potential clients. Just be sure to make a notation on the back of their cards so you'll remember why you're pursuing the relationship.

Another way to exhibit is by using a panel tabletop display. As the name implies, it sits right on the table, leaving you space to display brochures or other handout materials. These displays come in several configurations and run about $895, excluding the cost of the graphics.

This probably sounds pretty pricey, especially for a startup operation, but if you're planning to attend many bridal shows, the investment is worth it in terms of the professional image you'll project.

Bright Idea

Some wedding consultants package all their promotional and sales materials in a media kit, which can be given out to business prospects. Some of the items in the kit (usually organized in a pocket folder) may include a letter thanking clients for their interest, a "backgrounder" and other news releases, a brochure, and the owner's biography and photograph.

Another way to attract show attendees to your booth is by holding a drawing for a wedding-themed gift. For instance, you might invite visitors to fill out an entry form for a chance to win a pair of champagne flutes or a floral arrangement for the rehearsal dinner. One lucky winner takes home a gift (or a promissory note in the case of flowers), and you'll take home a bowl full of entry forms with the names and addresses of prospective clients. These prospects should immediately go on your mailing list so you can send them a newsletter you've developed especially for this purpose.

Packy Boukis, the Ohio wedding consultant, says she has found that bridal shows aren't always the best possible venue for attracting new business, but they still serve an important purpose. "Bridal shows give you visibility with the public, even if they don't generate a lot of business," she says. "They also give you a chance to meet and network with a lot of vendors all in one place."

Julia Kappel, the wedding consultant in Oak Point, Texas, concurs. She says, "Bridal shows are great—and I mean really great—for building credibility among vendors. We set up our booth an hour or two early before the other vendors, then go around and offer snacks and assistance to those who are scrambling to finish in time. They would get a chance to see firsthand how we can make their lives easier the day of the wedding and would begin recommending us without actually having worked with us at a wedding before."

Facebook and Twitter

These popular social networking tools were already discussed in detail in Chapter 10. But it bears repeating here that both Facebook and Twitter have huge public relations potential for aspiring bridal consultants. You can use these connection tools to:

- Comment on the newest trends in bridal fashion and fun
- Inform brides about wedding dress trunk shows and other events
- Critique destination wedding sites you've visited
- Establish your personal brand using your Twitter handle
- Look for temporary/contract employees
- Monitor media outlets to find out what types of information and sources they need so you can volunteer your knowledge bank
- Follow the media outlets on your mailing list so you can keep it updated
- Join a PR chat to talk about what works for service industries like yours
- Let people know where to find you on a given day, like at a bridal show

Beware!

Everyone knows the unwitting part Twitter played in the confrontation between Congresswoman Gabrielle Giffords and her would-be assassin in January 2011 in a Tucson parking lot. If you plan to tweet your whereabouts to followers, make sure you're not too specific about your exact location, or as a safety precaution make sure there are plenty of people around you.

Establishing a Facebook page or setting up a Twitter account is simple and easy. Just be sure that if you make the commitment to communicate with brides through social media you keep the page updated and the tweets coming. That's the only way to keep the excitement level high and your brand top of mind.

Networking

You know the old saying: "It's not what you know, but who you know." Well, it holds true. The more people you know in the wedding industry, the easier it will be to locate and land new business.

Two extremely valuable networking sources are your local chamber of commerce and Rotary Club. These organizations consist of both small- and large-business owners, and encourage their members to exchange ideas, support each other's businesses, and barter services. The cost to join either organization is reasonable, and you can quickly build a reputation as a caring and reputable business owner by becoming involved in the groups' public service activities.

You might also consider joining other professional business organizations in your area, such as economic clubs or women business owners' groups. Then get involved in the leadership of the group. That way, your name will be top of mind when one of the members is looking for or knows someone who needs a wedding consultant.

Finally, professional wedding consultant organizations are a good place to meet other planners and share tips and techniques. Many of the national organizations have regional chapters that hold regular meetings.

12

Matrimonial Money Matters

By now, you should be pretty jazzed about becoming a wedding consultant and feel like you're ready to take on the world one wedding at a time. But there's one itty bitty little thing you still have to work on because it can mean the difference between startling success and abysmal failure. We're talking, of course, about financial management.

Alas, this is the point where many people turn pale because let's face it: Financial management is not for everyone. But maybe you're one of the lucky ones. Maybe you excelled in math and accounting in school, so you're not fazed by the thought of balance sheets and cash flow statements. Or maybe you earned a bachelor's degree in business administration in a previous life and find the real challenge in this job to be soothing weepy brides or dealing with prima-donna vendors.

> **Smart Tip** Tip...
>
> Three measures of your business's ability to make a profit are the gross profit margin, operating profit margin, and net profit margin. Bankers will look at these ratios to determine how profitable your business is because without profits, you're not considered a good financing risk.

But if you're like many wedding consultants, who are long on enthusiasm, creativity, and common sense, and perhaps a wee bit short on financial acumen, don't despair—help is available. You just have to know where to look for it.

This chapter covers the types of financial reporting documents you must have for your consulting business, as well as an overview of the many expenses you're likely to incur in your startup phase.

Key Financial Statements

Back in Chapter 5, you read about the value of a professional accountant who can help you handle the myriad tasks required to keep a small business on track and in the black. But even if you take that advice to heart, you still need to know enough about your business finances so you know exactly where you stand, and so you understand the financial moves your accountant will recommend to keep the business healthy and growing.

So here's a look at the various financial statements every small-business owner needs to stay informed and make informed financial decisions:

- *Profit and loss statement (also called the P&L or income statement)*. The P&L statement depicts a company's financial performance by capturing operating results for a specific period of time, usually quarterly or annually. It shows the revenues and expenses generated by the company, which are tallied to indicator net profits or losses.

- *Balance sheet*. This worksheet is a snapshot of how your company is doing at any given time. It shows what your company owns (its assets and cash), what it owes (its liabilities), and the value of the business (its net worth, which is determined by subtracting liabilities from assets). A balance sheet must be generated and reviewed frequently—typically monthly or quarterly—so you always know how the business stands.

- *Cash flow statement.* This document is a record of how much money is coming into the business and how much is going out, both actual and anticipated. It's generated on a monthly, quarterly, or annual basis.

Savvy business owners review these financial documents on a regular basis,

Smart Tip
According to the SBA, most business owners don't realize that financial statements have a value that goes far beyond their use to prepare tax returns or loan applications. Using numbers as navigation aids can steer you in the right direction and help you avoid costly "breakdowns." That's great advice for anyone who wants to succeed as a small-business owner.

both to revel in how well their company is doing and to make any course corrections needed to keep the Good Ship Small Business afloat. You can use accounting software like Intuit QuickBooks and Sage Peachtree Accounting Software to generate your own financial statements, or leave the task in the capable hands of your accountant.

You'll find a sample P&L statement on page 133 that shows the operating costs for two hypothetical wedding consulting businesses: one that's homebased, and another that operates out of a small commercial space. They provide a rundown of the typical expenses a homebased wedding consultant can expect to incur. A P&L worksheet has been included for you on page 134 so you can estimate the costs for your own business as you read this chapter.

Smart Tip
It is always a good idea to keep separate accounts, one for personal use and one for your wedding consultant business expenses. Use a separate checking account as well as separate credit cards for all of your business expenditures. This will help to ensure accurate record-keeping and prove extremely helpful when tax season arrives.

Income and Operating Expenses

Rent or Mortgage Payment

Although it's recommended that you launch your wedding consulting business as a homebased enterprise, we recognize that some new business owners will prefer to project an image of über-professionalism by operating out of a commercial location. If that's your plan, the rent or mortgage expense has the honor occupying the first line on your P&L

Also, you'll have to include a figure for utilities (if they're not covered under your lease) and the maintenance of your office space (cleaning, trash removal, and so on). On the sample P&L, it's assumed that the utilities are included in the lease payment, but the business owner is paying $100 a month for office cleaning.

Telecommunication Expenses

A dedicated business telephone line is a must for a wedding consultant. Some wedding consultants prefer to use a cell phone for all business calls, but ask yourself: Do you really want prospective brides ringing you up for information about weddings that are 18 months away while you're trying to calm a nervous bride who's on the verge of hysteria because of some wedding day malfunction? And yes, there's voice mail for such calls, but how will you distinguish them from the wedding day calls you need to take right now? So install a traditional landline in your office and let voice mail pick up the calls that can wait.

If you're really on a shoestring budget and absolutely can't afford a second phone line, make sure you keep written records of the business calls made on your personal phone line. Uncle Sam requires written proof backing up your claim that a percentage of the phone cost is business related. You'll just have to do a little math to determine the percentage of the bill that relates to business usage. Or better yet—just cave in, get that second line, and save yourself some trouble.

An estimated charge of $30 per month for a landline that includes caller ID, voice mail and call waiting, as well as $40 a month for a business cell phone, have been included on the sample P&L.

Postage

Not everyone is willing to open email attachments, so from time to time you'll probably have to mail wedding services contracts to clients, confirmation letters to vendors, and possibly direct mail pieces to prospective clients. So be sure to allot some funds for monthly mailing costs on your P&L.

In addition, if your business is homebased, it's a good idea to rent a post office box, or

Bright Idea

Need to view, edit, and create Word, Excel, and other documents while on the go? There's an app for that, of course. Both QuickOffice (www.quickoffice.com) and Documents to Go (www.dataviz.com) allow you to edit email attachments and view pdf files, too. The apps work on smartphones, iPad, iPod touch, and more.

Sample Profit/Loss Statement—Startup Expenses

Here are sample income/operating expenses statements for two hypothetical wedding consulting businesses that reflect typical operating costs for this industry. "Weddings by Jamie Lynn" is the homebased business that averages 12 weddings per year. "Cherished Moments in Time" handles 20 to 30 weddings per year and operates out of a small space in a commercial building. You can compute your own projected income and expenses using the worksheet on page 134.

	Weddings by Jamie Lynn	Cherished Moments in Time
Projected Monthly Income	$2,085*	$5,200**
Projected Monthly Expenses		
Mortgage/rent	$0	$500
Utilities	$0	$0
Maintenance	$0	$100
Phone (landline)	$30	$30
Cellular service	$40	$40
Postage/P.O. box	$30	$50
Office supplies	$20	$20
Licenses	$0	$0
Insurance	$100	$400
Owner salary	$0	$1,000
Employee/contractor wages	$60	$665
Benefits/taxes	$0	$0
Advertising	$100	$500
Legal services	$6	$22
Accounting services	$0	$150
Transportation	$100	$250
Loan repayment	$0	$150
Online service	$40	$40
Web hosting	$5	$5
Miscellaneous expenses	$50	$100
Total Expenses	**$581**	**$4,022**
Projected Monthly Net Income	**$1,504**	**$1,178**

*10 weddings per year billed at $2,500 each
**25 weddings per year billed at $2,500 each

Profit/Loss Statement—Startup Expenses Worksheet

Item	Cost
Projected Monthly Income	$
Projected Monthly Expenses	$
Mortgage/rent	$
Utilities	$
Maintenance	$
Phone (landline)	$
Cellular service	$
Postage/P.O. box	$
Office supplies	$
Licenses	$
Insurance	$
Owner salary	$
Employee/contractor wages	$
Benefits/taxes	$
Advertising	$
Legal services	$
Accounting services	$
Transportation	$
Loan repayment	$
Online service	$
Web hosting	$
Miscellaneous expenses	$
Total Expenses	$
Projected Monthly Net Income	$

a mailbox at a mailing center like Mail Boxes Etc. or The UPS Store, to keep your business and personal mail separate and your home address private. Expect to pay $15 to $20 per month for a small- to medium-sized box.

Office Supplies

This includes all the paper clips, stationery, business cards, and other supplies you need to do business every day. Obviously, some expenses like business printing won't be incurred every month, so use the figure you found when you priced your stationery and business cards, and divide it by 12. About $20 per month should cover everything.

Licenses

Your business license is probably the only license you'll need, unless you need a license from the local health department to bake wedding cakes or provide other food you've prepared (including edible favors). A business license is usually quite inexpensive—as little as $10 per year, depending on the jurisdiction. This cost was included on the startup worksheet in Chapter 6, but a line is included on the P&L because licensing requirements vary, and the cost of more expensive licenses should be divided by 12 and recorded here.

Insurance

As discussed in Chapter 5, you can have your pick of tons of business insurance. It all depends on your tolerance for risk. The types of insurance you may wish to consider include general liability, errors and omissions (really a good idea for professional service businesses), and business interruption.

In addition to the rider on your existing homeowner's insurance policy, or your business owner's insurance policy, you should include the cost to insure the primary vehicle you'll use to travel to weddings and business appointments. As with phone expenses, you'll have to track your business-specific expenses. So if you use your vehicle to transport the kids to soccer or to go shopping, you'll have to estimate what percentage of the car is actually used for your business, then apply that to your insurance cost to arrive at a useable number. One reliable way to do this that the IRS will find acceptable is to keep a simple mileage log. Office supply stores sell mileage logbooks that are small enough to stash in your glove compartment or a pocket of your visor.

Finally, if someone else in your household isn't carrying employer-provided health insurance, add it to your list since it's 100 percent deductible for self-employed persons. You'll just have to pay the premiums upfront.

For the purposes of the sample P&L, a monthly figure of $100 per month was used for the low-end business. The high-end business pays $400 a month, which represents $100 for professional liability insurance and $300 for major medical.

Owner Salary

Many small-business owners, including wedding consultants, decline to take a salary in the startup phase of their business to give it the best possible chance to survive. Of course, you can only work without a salary if you have sufficient savings to survive, or if you secure a business startup loan that will pay your expenses in the formative years of your business. On the sample P&L, the owner of Weddings by Jamie Lynn had sufficient savings to allow her to plow all her profits back into the business, while the owner of Cherished Moments in Time takes a modest $1,000 per month salary, for which she works hard to secure enough wedding business to cover both the salary and her business expenses.

Employee/Contractor Wages

It's assumed that you won't have employees on your payroll in the early days of your consulting business. But you probably will have to bring in contract help to assist with on-site wedding day management, clerical tasks in the office, and so on. Many wedding consultants pay their helpers $10 to $15 per hour, while some pay a minimum of $100 for a daylong event. Try hiring college students or young adults right out of high school (any younger and you'll have to worry about them trying to make the altar boys laugh during the blessing of the rings, or staging an impromptu toga party using the Battenberg lace table linens). Young adults are usually ecstatic to accept even the low-end wage, since jobs in fast food or retailing pay much less.

In general, it's best to do your own hiring rather than using an employment agency to provide temporary or leased employees. Agencies tack a hefty service fee (as much as 40 percent) onto the basic hourly rate you'll pay, which can quickly erode your profits. Instead, try placing a brief want ad in your local community newspaper. Since most people love weddings, you should get a respectable number of responses, which will give you a nice pool of applicants to choose from.

> ### Dollar Stretcher
> Community news-papers are an excellent tool for unearthing prospective employees. Not only are their classified rates quite reasonable, but they're also read by people who live right in the area where you do business. Their familiarity with your market area is a plus, and their proximity to your work site increases the chances they'll always be on time.

Also, don't overlook stay-at-home moms or retirees as prospective employees. Retirees in particular make wonderful employees—they're usually very happy to help out however they can. Just make sure they have the stamina to be on their feet for long periods of time. By the same token, make sure any moms you hire have a reliable babysitter so you're not left to juggle the demands of an edgy bride and 500 hungry guests all by yourself some Saturday night.

Fortunately, unless you hire full-time employees, you aren't required to pay any benefits or withhold federal taxes or FICA from workers' paychecks. The contractors themselves are responsible for ponying up with the Feds. However, the IRS requires you to file Form 1099-MISC for every contractor whose annual wages exceed $600.

On the sample P&L, both businesses use contractors from time to time. Cherished Moments' costs are much higher because its owner uses college students to answer the phone and set up appointments in her leased office space. On the wedding side, she averages two workers per wedding for five hours each; on the administrative side, she averages 16 hours a week. Because these workers are all contractors and earn less than $600 per year, there are not benefits/taxes to report on the P&L.

Advertising

Experts recommend earmarking 3 to 5 percent of your gross sales for advertising the business. In your first year, you won't have historical financial data to which to refer, so guesstimate your costs by multiplying the number of weddings you hope to handle in your first year by your package price, then taking a percentage of that figure. Among the advertising costs you'll want to include will be any print advertising or public relations activities (such as the cost of having your news releases written for you), and so on. For simplicity's sake, a figure of $100 and $500 has been used for each business on the sample P&L.

Legal Services

As you know from Chapter 5, a prepaid legal plan is an easy and fairly reasonable way to get the minimal legal services you're likely to need. Legal plans start at about $70 a year, to as much as $400, with the latter providing far more services. For startup businesses, a cost equal to about one-twelfth of $70 and $250 has been included on the sample P&L for the Weddings by Jamie Lynn and Cherished Moments, respectively.

Accounting Services

You can expect to pay $50 an hour and up for accounting services, with $300 an hour at the highest end. Call around to see what rate the market will bear in your area.

For the sample P&L, the low-end consulting business, Weddings by Jamie Lynn, has chosen to do her own accounting using QuickBooks, while the owner of the high-end business, Cherished Moments, has designated $150 a month for accounting services at startup.

Transportation

You're allowed to deduct mileage on your business tax return each year, but in the meantime, you have to spring for gas money, windshield wiper fluid, and other travel-related costs. If you work in a metropolitan area like New York, you will also have public transportation costs that can be penciled in on your profit/loss statement. The sample P&L businesses estimated their costs at $100 and $250.

Loan Repayment

Because the cost to start a wedding consulting business is usually pretty low, you may not need a loan at startup, unless you're one of those people mentioned earlier who doesn't have much in the bank to keep the bills paid until the business starts to flourish. (Don't forget that you'll be footing the vendor bills out-of-pocket until your brides pay you, so a certain amount of upfront money is mandatory.)

No matter what the source of the loan is—a credit card advance, home equity loan, loan from friends or family, and so on—you'll need to include the monthly payments on your P&L, like the owner of Cherished Moments did because she needed to equip her new office and have some operating funds available.

Online Service Fees

There are always price wars going on in the world of ISPs, so shop around to get the best deal. The least expensive service is dial-up, which costs about $7 a month for limitless use. Connections are faster than in the bad old days, but it still can be pokey for wedding consultants on a schedule. Well-known providers include NetZero and PeoplePC. DSL is faster and runs from $15 to $20 a month for unlimited usage. DSL providers to check out include Verizon and AT&T U-Verse.

Finally, broadband delivered by your cable TV provider is the fastest—and priciest—service. You'll pay about $40 a month, and once you've gone there, you'll never go back. Cable providers usually provide phone/TV/broadband service packages at a discount rate. One to check out if you're in its service area is Comcast, which offers a $99 monthly package called "Business Class Internet and Voice." The phone service uses VoIP technology, which stands for Voice over Internet Protocol, and you must commit for two years to get the discounted rate.

Beware!
The IRS takes a dim view of business owners who try to deduct personal expenditures as business costs, so if you're home-based, always keep detailed records about your business internet usage. Better still, spring for an internet account that's completely separate from the service used by your family—and scrupulously make sure it's an Angry Birds-free zone.

The sample P&L reflects the cost of speedy broadband service for both businesses.

Finally, the monthly cost of web hosting, which you'll need to power up your website, should be included on your P&L, too. Web hosting is a bargain at an estimated $4.99 a month.

Other Miscellaneous Expenses

Don't forget to add up things like the cost of your dry cleaning, which is deductible when you're working out of town, and the cost of any food, snacks, or incidentals (like hairspray, panty hose, etc.) that you provide to the bridal party.

Receivables

If all is right with the world, the money you receive from your clients will offset all the operating expenses you just read about. Hopefully, you'll have a little change to jingle in your pocket after paying all the bills. But the only way you'll know where you stand is if you keep careful records of your receivables.

You can either design your own Excel spreadsheet to track receivables or use an accounting program like QuickBooks to keep an accurate running total. You'll find more information about accounting software later in this chapter.

Billing Your Clients

Most of the wedding consultants interviewed for this book bill incrementally for their services. Typically, they require payment for the consultation on the spot, then expect monthly payments for weddings that are planned over a very long period of time (like nine months to a year). Weddings that have a shorter lead time may be billed in two installments: one at the time of the contract and a second final payment 30 days after the event—or better still, right before the wedding just so no one "forgets" to settle up the bill.

Cancellations are not uncommon in this business, and Loreen Crouch, the wedding consultant in Michigan, tries to keep hers to a minimum by refunding just half the deposit if the cancellation occurs within seven days. After that, the deposit is forfeited.

"I have to do that because I might have turned someone else down for the same date," she explains.

It has become quite common for wedding consultants to have merchant accounts, which allow them to bill their clients' credit cards. Despite the merchant fees, which can be rather high for the merchant (that's you), offering a credit card option is a good idea since the cost to host a wedding tends to be rather high, too, and you'll be paying those costs out-of-pocket until you're paid. For this reason, even a brand-new wedding

> ## Smart Tip
>
> Always prepare a written contract that spells out your responsibilities and payment terms, since under the Uniform Commercial Code, contracts for the sale of services or goods in excess of $500 must be in writing to be legally enforceable. Even if your bill will be under $500, it's a good idea to have a written contract just in case a dispute arises.

consultant should consider establishing a merchant account right out of the gate. Check out the sidebar on page 141 for a rundown on what you can expect to pay for the privilege of accepting plastic.

If you plan to accept checks, you'll need a check validation service to guarantee that you won't be dribbling the checks all the way to the bank. Fees include a per-check discount fee (usually around 1.5 percent, according to MerchantSeek.com), a per-transaction fee (usually 10 to 35 cents), and possibly a monthly minimum fee, a statement fee, and an application fee. Despite the raft of fees, the peace of mind you'll gain is worth the cost.

Electronic Bookkeeping

One of the must-have tools for keeping a handle on your business finances is business accounting software. The hands-down choice of the wedding professionals interviewed for this book was Intuit QuickBooks Pro (www.quickbooks.intuit.com). This nimble, easy-to-use software allows you to create invoices, track receivables and expenses, write checks and pay bills, and more. It interfaces with Microsoft Word, Excel, and other software, and interfaces with QuickBooks Merchant Service. Another to try: Sage Peachtree (www.peachtree.com). Or feel free to use or adapt the sample invoice shown on page 142.

Where the Money Is

Now you have all your ducks in a row, and they're ready to quack. Your business plan is exemplary, and you have solid evidence that your community or metropolitan

A Plastic Fee-for-All

These days, it's become pretty much mandatory to accept credit and debit cards as a form of payment for wedding consulting fees. All you need is a merchant account, which is an account established with a bank or other payment processor for the purpose of accepting and clearing credit and debit card payments, and credit card processing equipment. But beware—merchant account providers slap a staggering number of fees on unsuspecting merchants. Here's a list of the fees you might be asked to pay, according to the merchant account provider Merchant Express (www.merchantexpress.com):

- Discount rate
- Transaction fees
- PIN debit transaction fees
- Address verification service fee
- ACH fee or daily batch fee
- Monthly statement/support/service fee
- Internet gateway fee
- Voice authorization fee
- Monthly minimum fee
- Surcharge/partially-qualified/non-qualified fees
- Application/setup fee
- Reprogramming fee
- Chargeback/retrieval fee
- Annual fee
- Cancellation or termination fee
- Hidden or junk fees

This is the Crazy Fee List—you'd be crazy to pay all of them. Fees that are reasonable to expect include a monthly statement fee ($10 to $15), a retail discount rate around 1.69 percent (meaning you pay the merchant account company 1.69 percent of each transaction), and a retail transaction/batch fee (about 19 cents per transaction). In addition to Merchant Express, you'll find a list of other merchant account providers in the Appendix you can check out. The bank where you do your business banking probably also offers merchant services that deserve a look.

Invoice for Wedding Consultant Business

 # Cherished Moments

25771 Waterloo Drive
Lake Buena Vista, Florida 00003

June 23, 20xx   Terms: Net 30

Sold To:

Cathy Russell
49855 Petrucci Drive
Clinton Township, FL 00003

Full service "Wedding Extravaganza"
consulting/coordination package $3,000

Russell/Roberts Nuptials

June 13, 20xx

TOTAL   **$3,000**

Thank You!

area has the well-heeled economic base necessary to support your fledgling business. So financing should be a snap, right?

In your dreams. Small-business owners sometimes find it's pretty hard to find a bank willing to work with them. This is usually because the mega rich banks are far more interested in funding large companies that need large amounts of capital. They're also leery about dealing with one-person and startup companies that don't have a long track record of success. So you may have trouble finding banking services like financing and merchant accounts that meet your small-business needs.

One way around this problem is to shop around to find a bank that will welcome the opportunity to work with you. "Small-business owners usually do better by selecting a bank with a community banking philosophy," says Robert Sisson, author of *Show Me the Money* (Adams Media). "These are the banks that support their communities and function almost as much as a consultant as a bank."

You probably already have a pretty good idea what the smaller banking players are in your community. Start by checking out their annual reports (which you can usually find online or at branch offices) for clues about their financial focus and business outlook. Important clue: Institutions that support minority- and women-owned businesses as well as small businesses are likely to be more willing to help your business. Next, look for information about the number of loans they make to small companies. That's a pretty good indicator of their community commitment. Finally, study their overall business mix and the industries they serve.

> ## Smart Tip Tip...
>
> According to the SBA's Small Business Development Center, all banks use certain key factors to determine a business's creditworthiness. These criteria include: collateral (assets to secure the loan), capital (owner's equity), conditions (anything that affects the financial climate), character (personal credit history), and cash flow (ability to support debts, expenses).

While it's not impossible to find a big bank that will welcome you into the financial fold, it's actually far more likely that a warm welcome will come from a smaller financial institution. Small banks are always looking for ways to accommodate small-business customers. As a result, they're usually more willing to deal with small-business concerns and are more sensitive to issues like the need for longer accounts receivable periods.

Uncle Sam to the Rescue

Even if you do find a bank friendly to small businesses, you may still have trouble establishing credit or borrowing money as a startup business. Banks, both large and small, are always more reluctant to part with their cash when the business owner doesn't have a proven track record of success.

That's where agencies like the SBA can help. The SBA offers many free services to small-business owners, including counseling and training seminars on topics like business plan or marketing plan development. The idea is to help owners understand what the bank will want from them before ever setting foot inside the front door, thus improving the chances of being approved for a loan or other financial services.

Self-Financing 101

Financing your wedding consulting startup with your personal credit cards can save you both the hassle of applying for a bank loan and the hefty costs that can be associated with it. Of course, the downside is that you'll probably pay interest rates of as much as 24.9 percent. So if you decide to use plastic, use a card with the lowest interest rate.

If your credit is good, you may be able to obtain a separate small-business line of credit through your credit card company. This allows you to borrow as much as $25,000, with no cost other than an application fee, and at a rate that's probably a lot less than what your bank would charge for a similar line of credit. American Express and Citibank are among the credit card companies that offer a small-business line of credit.

Although lending has tightened up significantly in recent years, tapping into the equity in your home could be another good way to secure funding. Just remember that your house is the collateral for the loan, and if the business doesn't do well and you can't make the payments, you could lose your home. In addition, there are restrictions on how you can use home equity funds. Business startups are usually viewed as risky propositions, so the bank may not be willing to hand over the cash. Still, a home equity line of credit is a viable option for some borrowers.

Although the SBA itself doesn't lend money, it serves as a sponsor, of sorts, for a number of different loan programs, counseling, and training. For more information, check the SBA's website at www.sba.gov, or call the answer desk at (800) 8-ASK-SBA (800-827-5722).

DIY Financing

Even with all the financing options out there, some newly established wedding consultants prefer to whip out their plastic to buy office equipment, pens, staplers, and the other goodies that make the business go. Others rely on loans from friends and family. But no matter what you do, make sure the process is handled in a professional, businesslike way. If you borrow from loved ones, sign a promissory note that details repayment terms and an equitable interest rate. Nothing can break up a tight-knit family faster than a broken promise of repayment or a misunderstanding of how the repayment will be handled. Your new business is important, but your family is precious. Protect it just like you would your business assets.

If you use your personal credit cards, watch your expenses closely. You can easily put yourself thousands of dollars in debt if you are not careful. Start out with the bare minimum whenever possible so your business will have a chance to grow and prosper without the specter of debt hanging over it.

13

Living Happily Ever After

In Chapter 1, we mentioned how wedding consultants make dreams come true for happy couples. We know you have your own dream: owning a successful business that allows you to do something you love. It is our hope that all your plans and hard work pay off, and you enjoy both happiness and longevity in your newly chosen career. But while we do wish you the best as you embark on this exciting new venture, we must acknowledge that every new business owner faces pitfalls that could threaten his or her company.

According to studies by the SBA Office of Advocacy, there were 27.5 million small businesses (defined as having fewer than 500 employees) in the United States in 2009, the last year for which data is available. They employ more than half the private work force and pay 43 percent of the total U.S. private payroll. What's more, they accounted for 65 percent (or 9.8 million) of the 15 million net new jobs created over the last two decades.

 **Beware!**

Avoid using vendors who are friends or family of the bride and groom. As Julia Kappel, the wedding consultant in Oak Point, Texas, says, "Many family and friends offer assistance or services out of the goodness of their heart and see the service as a favor or gift to the couple. But favors and gifts do not rank very high on the commitment scale of most people."

Sounds promising for the success of your new business, doesn't it? But let's do a reality check here. The SBA says that the average rate of business failure in the United States is about 10 percent, while the U.S. Census Bureau says that 99.9 percent of business closures occur among small companies. In fact, some small businesses don't make it through the first year.

Why Businesses Fail

Surveys by agencies like the SBA have shown that the reasons for these failures are numerous. Business failures can be due to market conditions (such as competition or increases in the cost of doing business), financing and cash flow problems, poor planning, mismanagement, and a host of other problems. Wedding consultants in particular are susceptible to additional difficulties fostered by poor communication, bad vendor relations, and underpriced services.

This is why it's strongly recommended that you hire professionals like attorneys, bookkeepers, accountants, and contract employees to assist you in the proper management and operation of your business. Because no matter how enthusiastic, knowledgeable, and bright you may be, you're probably not an expert in every field, and your time will stretch only so far. In the beginning, it can be pretty hard to part with the cash to pay those professional fees, but in the long run, it's worth it because this kind of help will allow you to focus your attention on the things you do best, rather than spend a lot of time doing things you are less proficient at.

And by the way, the outlook for success in a new business isn't completely bleak. Statistics suggest that the longer you're in business, the better your chances are of

Beware!

The SBA reports that too many small-business owners in financial straits don't call for help until it's too late to salvage their company. Don't fall into this trap. If you ever need help, call the SBA, which can provide advice and direction, or act as a loan guarantor. There's no charge for this service, and it could save everything you've worked so hard for.

staying afloat. Although the U.S. Census Bureau says that 30 percent of new businesses are not in business after two years, at least half of them are still in business after five years, and 25 percent will stay in business 15 years or more. Your task as a small-business owner is to do everything you can to help your business make it into that latter group.

Hindsight Is 20/20

Nearly every wedding consultant interviewed for this book readily admitted there were things he or she would do differently if it were possible to start again. For instance, Julia Kappel, the wedding consultant in Oak Point, Texas, says she would have selected a partner who was more committed.

"I ran the daytime activities, and she ran the evening activities because she chose not to give up her daytime job," Kappel says. "That meant she was working way too many hours in total, and I felt compelled to take more and more of her work so she could have some downtime every week. If I did it over, I would insist that both my partner and I were equally committed to doing only the wedding consulting so neither of us was too overworked."

Paula Laskelle, a wedding consultant in San Clemente, California, thinks she started out meeting the vendors in the industry too slowly, and if she had to start over, would speed up that process since that's the way to get a handle on the industry.

Lisa Michael in Bozeman, Montana, would have advertised more, something she didn't do much of in the early days because of the constraints of her initial budget. She also would have revamped her prices sooner, something she did (with much success) after she realized that people who came for the free introductory meeting didn't book her because her prices didn't fit the area she serves.

Smart Tip *Tip...*

Always draw up a contract for your clients outlining the services you've agreed to provide and the cost to provide them. Your attorney can help you draw up a standard contract that will cover most situations. You also can find a sample letter of agreement at www.weddingsforaliving.com that you can use as is or customize for your own needs.

▲

But even though every wedding consultant can identify something he or she could have done better, in every case these intrepid entrepreneurs used creative thinking, hard work, and good old-fashioned determination to meet whatever challenges faced them. Obviously, this is a strategy that works. These consultants survived that scary first year, and some of them have been prospering for decades.

Was it a miracle they persevered in the face of economic uncertainties and other pressures? Definitely not. It's due more to having the right stuff and knowing how to use it. It's also due to being willing to go the extra mile, which often results in acquiring a reputation as a miracle worker when it comes to solving the crises that can crop up in the course of planning and executing a dream wedding fit for a princess.

Wedding Stories to Learn From

Being able to think fast and execute plans on the spot can mean the difference between an ecstatic bride and one who is inconsolable.

Saving the Day

Julia Kappel earned her wings as a wedding day angel when she came to the rescue of a bride whose bower of flowers didn't materialize. The bride, who hired Kappel to coordinate a wedding for 500 guests, insisted on using a florist friend to do the flowers. Because the bride was a liquor distributor, she bartered with the florist to provide $300 worth of liquor in exchange for the wedding day flowers. All of this was done without the benefit of a contract.

Two weeks before the wedding, Kappel learned that the florist had gone out of business and someone else had taken over. Of course, the new owner knew nothing about the floral order. So even though she wasn't officially in charge of the floral arrangements, Kappel sprang into action and persuaded the new owner to design the bouquets and reception arrangements without charge, using flowers, glassware, and floral containers donated by two of her regular florist suppliers. Kappel donated candles from her own stock so the caterer could create decorations for the tables using donated rose bowls and hurricane lamps. All the product was delivered right to the reception site, and everything was completed in time for the reception.

"The amazing thing about all this was the original florist showed up before the wedding with a bucket of cheap leatherleaf greenery and started putting it into our arrangements," Kappel says. "We yanked it all out after he left."

Kappel credits her relationship with her vendors, her staff, and her own experience for being able to pull off such a feat on such short notice. She believes that if the client would have tried to solve this problem herself, the story probably wouldn't have had the same happy ending for all concerned—even for Kappel herself, who says, "This woman has sent us more referrals than anyone else I've worked with."

The Case of the Disappearing Guests

It's not unusual for summer showers or winter flurries to put a damper on a carefully planned wedding. But Lisa Michael in Montana had to fight the forces of nature to pull off the nuptials on one memorable summer day.

Michael was engaged to coordinate wedding day activities for a ceremony that was scheduled to take place on U.S. Forest Service land. Unfortunately, three days before the wedding, the Forest Service closed all the parks in the state of Montana because of the extreme threat of fire danger. The bride managed to locate an alternate site on private land about five miles up the road, but there wasn't enough parking to accommodate all the guests. So Michael had to make arrangements to bus the guests to the new site instead.

"Apparently there was some confusion about where the new place was because at 5:15 P.M. we still had no guests for the 5:30 P.M. ceremony!" Michael says. "I had brought my husband along to assist me that day, so I sent him up the road to look for the bus. The driver had gone about a mile past the turn and was starting to wonder where he had gone wrong. The guests were so happy to be rescued, they started applauding. I was glad I was there to worry about the guests so the bride and the mother-of-the-bride could enjoy the day."

Butterflies Aren't Free

Imagine having $2,000 worth of insects in your foyer—on purpose. That's what happened to Packy Boukis, the Ohio wedding consultant, when a bride (who happened to be a family member) asked her to arrange for a butterfly release after the ceremony.

"That's why brides hire you—to give them ideas that are different and to choreograph everything," Boukis says. "So I suggested the butterflies and had them delivered to my house before the wedding. I would never send them to the church because someone could put them by the heat accidentally and kill them. Luckily they come boxed in small triangle-shaped packets and were shipped on ice because I didn't want to touch them!"

Packy Boukis' butterfly release went off without a hitch, but it's important to note that releasing butterflies is actually detrimental to both the environment and the butterflies themselves. According to the North American Butterfly Association, releasing butterflies outside their natural habitat (e.g., any place to which they've been shipped in those little individual containers) confuses them and may cause them to expire prematurely (ironic given the symbolism of a wedding as the beginning of a new life together). An artificial release also can cause an inappropriate genetic mixing of species, which endangers them as a species even more.

If a bride loves the look and symbolic meaning of butterflies soaring skyward, encourage her to have her guests throw serpentines instead. These colorful paper streamers unfurl prettily when gently tossed, and because they're easily swept up afterward, there's no environmental impact. Best of all, you'll be saving the lives of hundreds of grateful Monarchs.

Head Over Heels

Loreen Couch, the Michigan wedding consultant, always takes a tool kit with personal supplies for the bride, as well as a utility kit full of tools for herself, to every wedding she coordinates. But one of the things she didn't used to pack was super bonding glue. That is, until a mishap with a cake brought the omission to her attention.

"While we were setting up for a reception, the DJ hit the cake table with a cord," Couch says. "The cake topper fell off the cake, and the groom's head came right off. I bring a lot of extra things with me, but I never have a backup cake topper. I also didn't have any super glue."

But the quick-thinking wedding consultant did have nail glue in her purse, so while her assistant smoothed out the frosting on the top layer of the cake, Couch reattached the groom's little head and no one was the wiser. "I sure never said a word about it!" she says.

Speaking of coming to the rescue, that's the idea behind the tool kits Couch brings along on wedding days. Some of the things in her tool kit (besides super glue) are a hammer, nails, screwdriver, tape, tape measure, decorator straight pins (for tasks like attaching lights to tablecloths or pinning ivy), wire cutters, extension cord, glue gun, rope (presumably not to use on a reluctant groom), and office supplies. The bride's customized kit contains things of a more personal nature, such as Tylenol, antacid, ginger ale, panty hose, mints, face powder, body lotion, lip gloss, makeup, perfume, hairspray, and a small water cup. Couch says, "I have each bride fill out a little survey in advance so I know her preferences and sizes when I put her customized kit together."

Ants for the Memory

Julia Kappel had her own close encounter with a wedding cake when she was supervising a rehearsal at an old mansion, while a reception for a different wedding was being set up in another room. "I happened to look into the empty room, when I passed by and noticed the cake," Kappel says. "From a distance, it looked like parts of it were moving, so I went in for a closer look and saw it was covered with thousands of ants."

Neither the caterer nor—luckily—the bride were anywhere in sight. So even though she was not coordinating that particular wedding, Kappel calmly removed the top layer of the cake, which mercifully was untouched by the bugs, sprayed the rest of the layers with bug spray, and blew off the dead insects. She then made arrangements with a local grocery store to provide sheet cakes free of charge that could be served instead of the ruined cake.

"In the South, the cake is usually cut in front of the guests, but this time it was wheeled into the kitchen so no one ever knew a thing," Kappel says. "This kind of

Signs of Success

You now know about the red flags that can signal a business failure. So what are the signs that your wedding consulting business will be successful?

1. You are providing a useful service at a price the market can bear.

2. Your local business market has enough customers to support your business.

3. You have enough savings or financing to weather the three-year make-or-break period.

4. Your business and marketing plans are sound, and you know where to go if you need help implementing them.

5. You have a good team of support service providers.

6. Your top priority is providing great customer service to your brides.

7. You keep careful records and always know where your business stands financially.

8. You're always aware of what your competition is up to.

9. You're flexible enough to change your business strategy when the situation warrants it.

10. You truly love your job and can't imagine doing anything else!

problem with insects actually is more common in the South than you might think because of the heat and humidity. So I insisted the facility spray for bugs the next day so I didn't have problems with my wedding, too."

Your Formula for Success

It's easy to see that the kind of flexibility exhibited by Kappel and the other consultants mentioned in this chapter is one of the hallmarks of being a professional in this field. "You can't be a dramatic person in this business," Kappel stresses. "You also can't let the bride see that you're upset. You have to smile when you're upset, or when you're dressing down a vendor, or when you're worried because a car hit a utility pole and knocked out the power two hours before the reception. You have to be fast on your feet and even faster than the bride."

You also have to be very committed to making your business a success. "We don't go on vacation," says Jenny Cline, a wedding consultant in Texas. "Every day is an adventure as it is!"

Organization and mediation skills rank high on Couch's personal list of required skills. "A lot of times you have to step in and keep the peace because the family wants something one way, while the bride and groom want it another way," she says. "Other times you have to put your foot down and stand firm so everything goes right."

Success in this business also comes from taking advantage of every opportunity that comes along. For instance, Couch had magnetic signs the size of bumper stickers made up that say, "Planning a Wedding?" and give her website address. She affixes them to the bumper of her car whenever she goes out for a spin, and at about $12 each, they are a very inexpensive way to advertise her services.

Couch also hands out her business card lavishly as a way to generate new leads. "If I go to the bank and the teller is wearing an engagement ring, I give her a card," she says. "I'm always looking at women's left hands."

Finally, patience is a virtue that every consultant we spoke to cited as critical for success. "You have to be patient, both with your clients and your business, because each wedding you're hired for will require different things of you," Michael says.

Beware!
Never pass yourself off as an expert in an area with which you're not completely familiar. Robbi Ernst III of June Wedding says, "Your client is paying for professional as well as creative talents. So if you don't have one of these creative talents, simply say so. Then rely on your well-chosen vendors to fulfill the need instead."

Super powers don't hurt, either. According to Nancy Tucker of Coordinators' Corner, being a first-rate wedding consultant means "having the talents of negotiation, mediation, and sometimes levitation!"

And it is exactly those skills, that variety, that challenge, and that desire for excellence that makes the wedding consulting business so vital and exciting. May you enjoy great success in your new venture, and may all your dreams and business wishes come true!

Appendix
Wedding Consultant Resources

There's a plethora of wedding consulting and small-business information available to assist you as you build your new business. Following is just a sampling of the many resources and tools out there. Please remember, though, that businesses move, change, fold, and reinvent themselves, so you may find that some of the information here has changed, too. A little creative browsing online will connect you to virtually anything you need to know to become a successful wedding consultant.

▲

Associations

American Academy of Wedding Professionals
(866) 648-2146
www.aa-wp.com

Association for Wedding Professionals International
www.afwpi.com

Association of Bridal Consultants (ABC)
(860) 355-7000
www.bridalassn.com

Association of Certified Professional Wedding Consultants (ACPWC)
(408) 227-2792
www.acpwc.com

June Wedding Inc. (JWI)
(707) 865-9894
http://jwidallas.org

National Black Bridal Association
www.nationalbba.com

National Bridal Service
(804) 342-0055
www.nationalbridal.com

SuperWeddings.com
www.superweddings.com

Weddings Beautiful Worldwide
www.weddingsbeautiful.com

Wedding Consultant Certification Institute
(678) 333-1130
www.weddingconsultantcertificationinstitute.com

The Wedding Planning Institute
www.theweddingplanninginstitute.com

WeddingSolutions
www.weddingsolutions.com

Attorney Referrals and Information

American Bar Association
www.abanet.org

Find an Attorney
www.findanattorney.us

Lawyers.com
www.lawyers.com

Martindale-Hubbell Law Directory
(800) 526-4902, option 2
www.martindale.com

Blogging Platforms

Blogger
www.blogger.com

WordPress
www.wordpress.com

Books for Further Reading

Colin Cowie Wedding Chic: 1001 Ideas for Every Moment of Your Celebration
Colin Cowie
Clarkson Potter

The Constant Contact Guide to Email Marketing
Eric Groves
Wiley

Destination Bride
Lisa Light
F&W Publications

The Destination Wedding Workbook
Paris Permenter and John Bigley
www.booklocker.com

Grace Ormonde Weddings
Grace Ormonde
Elegant Publishing

Great Wedding Tips from the Experts: What Every Bride Can Learn from the Most Successful Wedding Planners
Robbi Ernst III
McGraw-Hill

The Portable Wedding Consultant
Leah Ingram
McGraw-Hill

Tiffany Wedding
John Loring
Doubleday

Weddings by Martha Stewart
Martha Stewart
Clarkson Potter

Wedding Worries . . . and How to Put Them Right
Suzan St. Maur
How to Books

Bridal Shows and Information

Bridal Association of America
(877) 699-5884
www.bridalassociationofamerica.com

Bridal Show Producers International
(402) 330-8900
www.bspishows.com

Brides-to-Be Shows Inc.
(586) 228-2700
www.bridestobe.us

One Wed
www.onewed.com

Business Software

Intuit
www.intuit.com

Microsoft
www.microsoft.com

Catering Information

National Association of Catering Executives
www.nace.net

Demographic Information

American Fact Finder
www.factfinder2.census.gov

U.S. Census Bureau
www.census.gov

Disc Jockeys

American Disc Jockey Association
(888) 723-5776
www.adja.org

1-800-DISC JOCKEY
www.800dj.com

Educational Opportunities

Ashworth College
www.ashworthcollege.edu

Penn Foster Career School (Certified Wedding Planner program)
(800) 214-6230
www.pennfoster.edu

Employee and Vendor Issues

Better Business Bureau
www.bbb.org

U.S. Department of Labor
www.dol.gov

Flower Information

1-800-Flowers
www.1800flowers.com

FTD
www.FTD.com

Teleflora
www.teleflora.com

Limousines

Limos.com
www.limos.com

Limousine Directory
www.limousinedirectory.com

National Limousine Association
www.limo.org

Merchant Accounts

Capital Merchant Solutions Inc.
(877) 495-2419
www.takecardstoday.com

Credit Card Processing Services
(888) 717-1245
http://ccps.biz

InfoMerchant
(971) 223-5632
www.infomerchant.net

Total Merchant Services
(888) 871-4558
www.accept-credit-cards.com

Merchant Account Alternative

PayPal
www.PayPal.com

Newsletter Software

Design & Print Business Edition
www.avanquest.com and many office and electronic stores

Microsoft Publisher
www.microsoftstore.com and many office and electronic stores

Print Shop Professional
www.broderbund.com and many office and electronic stores

Office Equipment (Phones)

Hello Direct
(800) 435-5634
www.HelloDirect.com

Office Depot
www.officedepot.com

Office Max
www.officemax.com

Staples
www.staples.com

Office Supplies, Forms, and Stationery

Office Depot
www.officedepot.com

Office Max
www.officemax.com

Overnight Prints
www.overnightprints.com

Rapidforms
(800) 257-8354
www.rapidforms.com

Staples
www.staples.com

Vistaprint.com
www.vistaprint.com

Online Information Sources

Book More Brides
www.bookmorebrides.com

Brides
www.brides.com

Coordinator's Corner
www.coordinatorscorner.com

The Knot
www.theknot.com

Perfect Wedding Guide
www.perfectweddingguide.com

Premier Bride
www.premierbride.com

Wed Alert
www.wedalert.com

Online Postage

Pitney Bowes
www.pitneyworks.com

Stamps.com
www.stamps.com

USPS
www.usps.com

Zazzle
www.zazzle.com

Pay-Per-Click Advertising Resources

Google AdWords
www.adwords.google.com

Microsoft adCenter
https://adcenter.microsoft.com/

Yahoo! Search Marketing
http://searchmarketing.yahoo.com

Photographer Referrals

Professional Photographers of America Inc.
www.ppa.com

Publications

Advertising Age
www.adage.com

Bridal Guide magazine
www.bridalguide.com

Brides
www.brides.com

Destination Weddings & Honeymoons
www.destinationweddingmag.com

Event Solutions
www.event-solutions.com

Get Married **magazine**
www.getmarried.com

Southern Bride
www.southernbride.com

The SuperWeddings **newsletter**
www.superweddings.com

Today's Bride
www.todaysbrideonline.com

Vows
www.vowsmag.com

WedLock
(800) 318-5059
www.wedlockmag.com

Wedding Style **magazine**
www.weddingstylemagazine.com

Small Business Development Organizations

National Federation of Independent Business
www.nfib.com

Service Corp of Retired Executives (SCORE)
www.score.org

Small Business Association (SBA)
www.sba.gov

Small Business Development Centers
www.sba.gov

Tax Advice, Help, and Software

H&R Block
www.handrblock.com

Internal Revenue Service (IRS)
www.irs.gov

Intuit TurboTax for Business
www.turbotax.com

Trade Show Displays

Airworks Displays & Booths
(800) 900-9247
www.airwork.com

New World Case Inc.
(888) 883-0107
www.portablebooths.com

Pinnacle Displays
(800) 320-1466
www.pinnacledisplays.com

Siegel Display Products
(800) 626-0322
www.siegeldisplay.com

SmartExhibits.com
(800) 430-6111, (952) 448-3049
www.smartexhibits.com

Wedding and Event Videographers Association International
www.weva.com

Web Hosting/Domain Names

Domain.com
www.domain.com

EarthLink
www.earthlink.net

GoDaddy.com
www.godaddy.com

HostMonster
www.hostmonster.com

IPOWERWEB
www.ipowerweb.com

SBC Webhosting.com
www.webhosting.com

Yahoo!
http://yahoo.com

Wedding Cake Referrals

International Cake Exploration Societé
www.ices.org

Wedding Consultants

Packy Boukis, JWIC
Only You
www.clevelandwedding.com

Robbi G.W. Ernst III
June Wedding Inc.
http://jwidallas.org

Marsha Ballard French, MCWP, and Jenny Cline, CWP
Stardust Celebrations Inc.
www.stardustcelebrations.com

Donna M. Horner
Elegant Weddings by Donna
(512) 441-9235

Lisa Kronauer
Events By Studio K
info@eventsbystudiok.com

Paula Laskelle
Champagne Taste
www.weddingsbyct.com

Deborah McCoy
American Academy of Wedding Professionals
www.aa-wp.com

Ann Nola
Association of Certified Professional Wedding Consultants
www.acpwc.com

Nancy Tucker
Coordinators' Corner
www.coordinatorscorner.com

Wedding Planning Software

Event Magic Pro and Room Magic Pro
(866) 439-9617
www.frogware.com

iDo Wedding and Event Professional Edition
www.elmsoftware.com

My Wedding Workbook Professional Edition
www.myweddingworkbookpro.com

Wedding Management for Professionals
Murphy's Creativity Software
(619) 441-9664
www.weddingmanagement.net

Glossary

Backgrounder: a news release that gives general information about your business that will spur the local media to do a more in-depth story about your company and services.

Balance sheet: in financial parlance, the statement that shows a business's assets, liabilities, and net worth.

Blog: short for weblog, which is an online newsletter or journal, sometimes with multiple authors.

Blogosphere: an informal term that collectively refers to all of the weblogs (blogs) on the internet.

Cash flow statement: a financial document that tracks the cash paid by a company to its creditors.

Click-through: the process of clicking an internet advertisement (often found in a "Sponsored links" list, to go to an advertiser's website; also called "ad clicks."

Corporation: a separate legal entity distinct from its owners.

dba (doing business as): refers to your legal designation once you have selected a business name different from your own and registered it with your local or state government.

Demographics: the primary characteristics of your target audience, such as age, gender, ethnic background, income level, education level, and home ownership.

Domain name: the address of an internet network (for example, www.entrepreneur. com).

Executive summary: brief document at the beginning of a report, like a business plan, that summarizes its contents.

Facebook: a multimedia social networking website with profiles, photos, and videos created by the "owner" that contains a "wall" where friends and visitors can post messages.

Flash: a graphic animation that plays when a visitor first arrives at a website's home page.

Freelancer: a self-employed person who works on a project or contract basis to produce written materials or artwork for advertisements, brochures, or other printed materials (including news releases).

Gutter: in book publishing, the white space formed by adjoining pages of a book when they're bound together.

Hit: in internet parlance, a successful retrieval of information from a website.

Keywords: words inserted into electronic text that's posted on the internet for the purpose of helping a website rank higher in a search engine.

LLC: limited liability company.

LinkedIn: a business-oriented social networking site used for professional networking.

Logo (or logotype): an identifying symbol used by organizations (as in advertising).

Media kit: a packet that contains publicity and sales materials about a company and its services.

Merchant account: an account established with a bank or other payment processor for the purpose of accepting and clearing credit and debit card payments.

Mission statement: a brief summary telling who your company is, what you do, what you stand for, and why you do it.

Netbook: a small laptop computer used primarily to access content on the internet.

Newsletter: a marketing vehicle that contains short, newsy articles that promotes a business.

News release: also called "press release"; refers to a one- to two-page article about some positive aspect of your business meant to generate favorable publicity.

Partnership: a business owned equally by two or more persons, or partners.

Point of Sale (POS) terminal: an electronic transaction device used to verify that credit or funds are available when a customer makes a purchase.

Profit and loss statement: a financial document that tracks a company's revenues, costs, and expenses over a specific period of time. Also known as an income statement.

Retainer: money paid in advance for services rendered in the future.

Rider: an add-on provision to an existing insurance policy designed to protect against losses not covered by the standard policy.

RSS feed: an internet-based content delivery system; acronym stands for "Really Simple Syndication."

SCORE: the nation's premier source for free and confidential business advice for small-business owners; accessible at www.score.org.

Search engine: an internet program that searches documents for specific words designated by the person searching; Google, Bing, and Dogpile are examples of search engines.

SEO: acronym for "search engine optimization"; refers to the process of improving web page visibility on the internet through the use of keywords and other techniques.

SEP (or SEP IRA): Simplified Employee Pension plan; similar to an IRA, this tax-deferred savings plan has higher contribution limits (25 percent of business income); considered to be a qualified pension plan.

Social networking: using web-based tools to communicate with other people on the same site; Facebook and Twitter are examples of social networking sites.

Sole proprietorship: a business owned by one person (a sole proprietor).

Stock photo: a photograph that is licensed for general use by businesses or the public; most of the time, you'll pay a fee to use stock photos, although some are available online at no charge.

Telemarketing: using the telephone to generate new sales or leads.

Tussy mussy: a small floral nosegay designed in an antique bouquet holder.

Twitter: a social networking service over which users send short (140-character) messages to a select group of "followers"; messages are called "tweets."

Videographer: a person who videotapes an event like a wedding.

Viral marketing: marketing that encourages people to pass along a marketing message over the internet.

VoIP: acronym for Voice over Internet Protocol; technology that allows users to place telephone calls over the internet.

Web host: an internet-based service used to make websites accessible on the internet.

Index